EXPECT THE BEST

EXPECT THE BEST

The Philosophy Behind Tony Walker Financial

GARY P. WEST

P.O. Box 238
Morley, MO 63767
(573) 472-9800
www.acclaimpress.com

Book & Cover Design: Rodney Atchley

Copyright © 2023, Tony Walker Financial
All Rights Reserved.

No part of this book shall be reproduced or transmitted in any form or by any means, electronic or mechanical, including photocopying, recording or by an information or retrieval system, except in the case of brief quotations embodied in articles and reviews, without the prior written consent of the publisher. The scanning, uploading, and distribution of this book via the Internet or via any other means without permission of the publisher is illegal and punishable by law.

ISBN: 978-1-956027-54-9 / 1-956027-54-8
Library of Congress Control Number: 2023935236

First Printing 2023
Printed in the United States of America
10 9 8 7 6 5 4 3 2 1

This publication was produced using available information.
The publisher regrets it cannot assume responsibility for errors or omissions.

CONTENTS

Foreword. 6
Chapter One:
"It's hard to get a lot done when you're asleep." 10
Chapter Two:
"Whenever in doubt, always go with the fastball." 15
Chapter Three:
"Even if you're dead broke,
act like you've got enough money to buy the place." 21
Chapter Four:
"Never assume anything; things can change in a heartbeat." 26
Chapter Five:
"Don't look a gift horse in the mouth…
when opportunity presents itself, jump on it." 34
Chapter Six:
"Hard work beats dumb luck every time." 37
Chapter Seven:
"It is true; you really can't take it with you." 42
Chapter Eight:
"It never hurts to ask." 46
Chapter Nine:
"If you want something incredible,
find others with the ability to make it happen." 51
Chapter Ten:
"Nothing stays the same." 56
Chapter Eleven:
"In order to grow a business,
you must keep investing in yourself and in others around you." 61
Chapter Twelve:
"If you're having trouble finding the fairway, move up to the next tee." 98
Chapter Thirteen:
"Sometimes the best employees are right under your nose." 103
Chapter Fourteen:
"The most precious and difficult-to-find commodity in business? Honesty.". . 105
Chapter Fifteen:
"There's no such thing as a free lunch." 109
Chapter Sixteen:
"There's no point in saving money for the future
if you don't have a plan in place to spend it." 113
Chapter Seventeen:
"At the end of the day,
it's not about the money but about the journey, so never give up." 120
About the Author 125
Index 126

FOREWORD

Sometimes the timing just isn't right. This was the case when Tony Walker approached me several years ago about writing a book portraying his life.

At the time I was completely wrapped up in writing, not one, but two books, which precluded me from taking on another project.

Tony's notoriety as a successful financial guy, even then would have been a worthy addition to the previous eighteen books I had authored. However, the time just wasn't right no matter how much I wanted to do it.

I knew it was right when my phone rang one day in July 2022. It was Tony telling me he had been thinking this book thing over again and would like to meet with me about writing his story.

"But, but, but, Tony, I'm through with writing books. Eighteen is enough, and besides," I continued, "writing a book takes a lot out of you. But thank you for even asking," I said.

Tony Walker has been a friend of mine here in Bowling Green, Kentucky, for several years, so, of course, I told him we would get together. In my mind I had a plan.

As I walked into Tony's Bowling Green office, I was prepared to politely tell him my book writing days had come to an end, and although unlike several years before, now I didn't have any big projects going, but another book was not in my future.

"But Tony," I said, "you've written several books. You're a good writer. Why not you?"

It fell on deaf ears. "I want your perspective on it all," he quickly challenged. I found myself now listening as he briefly laid out an overview of his life and where he now was with his company, Tony Walker Financial.

For some thirty minutes I listened. As he talked my mind went from "I'm not writing this book," to "I can't wait to write this book."

Tony's a young man by "having old standards," but, he has a story to tell. Not only does he have a story, but it's one people will want to read.

Listening to Tony, I was amazed that just the few stories he told really piqued my interest and propelled me into his world and this book.

Tony's ability to relate to people, making them feel at ease, may be his greatest asset. His rise to success has not been without a setback here and there, and for sure he has had to keep the bugs off his windshield. He and his wife, Susan, have called on their faith throughout their marriage while making it a staple of their personal and business lives.

After several attempts, it took Tony a while to find his path in life. Early on he was determined to do one thing but found that path blocked. But it was not in his personality to give up. No, as you'll soon discover, Tony is one who has always believed in giving it 110%, no matter how difficult life might be nor the task at hand might seem.

Getting a "no" only made him more determined. It has been said one measure of intelligence is the ability to change. Give Tony a big plus for that.

—Gary P. West,
Author

EXPECT
THE BEST

Chapter One
"IT'S HARD TO GET A LOT DONE WHEN YOU'RE ASLEEP."

Tony Walker strolls confidently to his position in front of one of three cameras in his second-floor television studio at Tony Walker Financial in Louisville.

He and his WorryFree Productions team had just completed a pre-production meeting, going over how the taping of a few TV shows and a radio show would play out once the cameras were rolling.

Tony's financial business had skyrocketed over the last few years to the point that after opening his first office in Bowling Green, locations in Louisville and Lexington followed. Much of the growth can be attributed to television . . . his show.

From the outset, Tony knew that he wanted a first-class production with the best available people and the best equipment. It proved to be a wise decision when he invested six figures in set design, cameras, and lights.

The radio and television productions have become a major marketing arm for Tony Walker Financial, so much that he has two full-timers, whose main job is to take ideas Tony has and turn them into slick thirty-minute shows to be aired at a later date on radio and television throughout Kentucky.

Aaron Orrender produces the show. He's been with Tony as far back as when Tony's show originated out of WAVE TV in Louisville. When Tony decided to take his show in-house, Orrender became his number one man. As of October 2022, he had produced 435 Tony Walker Financial shows.

Deric Hudson rounds out the team, and together their TV and radio products have helped turn Tony Walker into a household name.

Tony takes care of his own script, generated many times at 3:45 a.m. "I've always said that it's hard to get a lot done when you're asleep . . . God has blessed me with the ability to work on limited amounts of it," he says.

A man of structure and routine in his business, the same can be said in his studio operation. His production meetings always revolve around keeping the message simple.

"We're actually not in the financial business," Tony says. "We're in the communication business. Most people don't understand money. The financial world talks over their heads. Our show deals in terms and on a level our viewers understand. The more they understand, the less they worry."

With the routine of the show engrained in Tony and the crew, still they leave nothing to chance. Scripts, graphics, teleprompter, camera angles, and lighting are all reviewed. The mood is relaxed, and even though Tony is in charge, he is quick to take suggestions that will make the show better.

Orrender positions himself in front of the camera, announces the episode and segment number, and in Hollywood style slams the clapperboard. It's lights, camera, action.

Tony is at ease . . . like he's done this before. "Rolling," says Orrender, "3-2-1," says Tony, doing the countdown.

In a helter-skelter sort of way, the production of the show runs smoothly. Tony is an expert at adjusting to the situation, and his two-person crew is equally up to the task.

"It's a team approach," Tony says later. "We anticipate each other, sort of like a basketball team playing defense."

From the outset, Tony is quick to establish that he is knowledgeable, and without a doubt an expert in the field of financials.

One thing he emphasizes loud and clear on every show is his credentials as a fiduciary. He explains the rigorous requirements a recipient must go through in order to meet these standards. He explains to viewers that the process of becoming a fiduciary is overseen by the Security and Exchange Commission, and by law he is obligated to work in the best interest of his clients.

Tony, during his tapings, never loses sight of making sure his presentation stays on a level that viewers can understand. There will be times when some of the content is changed on the fly to make sure he stays on message. It is not uncommon for him to bring in employees from the Bowling Green office, either by zoom or in studio in Louisville to explain their role and expertise in the company. Changing up the show as they go is not a distraction.

During a break, Tony and the crew will get their heads together as to how they can explain better to viewers the points they want to get across. "We want to make sure they understand what we are saying," says Tony.

The flow of the television productions go smoothly. Parts of the different episodes include Tony bringing in his "favorite son-in-law" (his only one), Trey Jurgens, to talk about whatever the days main topic is. Then he'll bring in his "favorite nephew" (his only nephew), Wes Walker.

Tony is working more of his staff into front-and-center roles to make sure viewers know there is more-than-able qualified personnel to handle their financial needs and concerns should Tony no longer be around.

As the show moves along, Aaron and Deric interact off camera with Tony. He is comfortable as he reads from the teleprompter and ad libs his way through the show, relying on his experience, knowledge, and verbal skills. Aaron is quick to respond to Tony's questions and comments. It's easy to see that he is a veteran of working with Tony.

With the cameras rolling, Tony will direct Aaron. "Let's go full screen, Aaron," or he might say, "Deric, put a graphic up on that."

Terms like annuities, commissions, and surrender charges are frequently discussed and explained. The use of annuities has become a big part of who Tony Walker Financial is. He talks about how an annuity is backed by an insurance company, and that an insurance company's priority is not to invest your money, but to protect it. He tells viewers how much commission is paid and who pays it. "When you buy an insurance policy of any kind, life, car, home, someone gets paid," he says to the camera.

Tony's TV show talks about Wall Street, and how its growth didn't really jump until 1978 when the 401(k) plan was enacted for the first time.

"Mutual funds today possess trillions of dollars inside of them because Savers have been led to believe this is the only way to grow your money and to enjoy retirement," he tells viewers.

Tony, on both his radio and television shows, refers to himself as the "little man in the sweater vest." Before each show he changes into a fresh collared, button-down shirt under one of his twelve black sweater vests with the Tony Walker Financial logo stitched on the upper left side.

The confidence Tony has in his production crew is evident by how much responsibility they have, and their ability to create little sidebar skits that inject humor while adding to the script.

Admitting that some of his best ideas for the show come to him in the wee hours of the morning, he is quick to get them on paper.

Tony is always thinking about how to make, not just his TV and radio productions better, but his entire operation better. He will only be limited to how far his imagination will take him.

To viewers who see the finished product, it all looks so together. It's sort of like the sausage you eat for breakfast. It sure does taste good, but you probably don't want to see how it's made.

For sure, Tony's TV company, WorryFree Productions, is not that extreme, but it does show how talented the crew is in turning two hours of pulling together a multitude of financial issues into a slick thirty-minute show. And if they are lucky, the audio content of the show can be used for the radio broadcast.

"We'll work three or four days to get the polished finished show," says Orrender.

Not to be overlooked is what Tony refers to as the "What the Bible has to say about money segment" of his show. Since the television shows are aired in Louisville, Lexington, and Bowling Green on Sundays, it makes sense for him to talk about his faith and his feelings about money and what God's word says. Tony truly believes that his take on life is a three-prong approach of "Man, Money, and God". As he likes to say, "True balance in life comes with an appreciation of all three."

Tony, away from rolling cameras, talks about and never forgets the down and out despair he went through when in 1991, he found God.

"It changed me, personally and in business," he says. "My faith is very important to me, and that's why I want to make it part of Tony Walker Financial. If I can play a small role in encouraging others to not give up on their faith in God, then it's all worth it."

However, Tony points out that not everyone agrees with his take on scripture. "But that's okay," he says. "However, one viewer I bumped into told me that each and every Sunday morning, he watched all the gloom and doom he could stand on the morning news just before our show comes on the air. Then he watches Tony Walker for some good news."

Reaching Tony's level of achievement has not been easy. To get to the success of this stage of his career he and wife Susan have traveled winding roads, climbed steep hills, and endured setbacks many families with three children would have given up on years ago, but together they have never quit.

Chapter Two
"WHENEVER IN DOUBT, ALWAYS GO WITH THE FASTBALL."

What a person does in life is, more often than not, determined by what their parents did. For Tony, and older brother Marty, it was no different.

Tony and Marty's father, Richard "Dick" Walker, was a social worker, and their mother, Jo, had left college after meeting Dick at a bowling class he was teaching at the University of Kentucky (UK), to marry him.

Dick grew up in Drakesboro, Kentucky, a mining community in Western Kentucky. His dad, Harry Walker, ran a general store located in the front of the family home. He, his wife, and their family of four girls and two boys lived in the back of the store. His customers were coal miners, and it didn't take Dick long to realize he had no desire to be a storekeeper, nor a coal miner. Dick had seen the hard life of tending to the needs of coal miners and the effects the hard labor of working the mines had on the folks in Drakesboro. The closest Dick got to hard labor was, as a young teenager, delivering large blocks of ice to homes around Muhlenberg County. Remember, this was a time before refrigeration was common.

Dick Walker, however, wanted a future. Even though his mother had become a schoolteacher later in life, teaching school was not in his cards either. Oh sure, as a graduate student at UK, he pretended to know something about bowling as he talked his way into teaching a bowling class to undergraduates. Tony recalls meeting one of his former students later as an adult who said he took Dick's bowling class at UK, and it was the only 100 he ever got at UK. In the meantime, Dick being musically inclined, parlayed his motivation to leave Muhlenberg County and his interest in going to college into a band scholarship at UK.

Being in the band at UK was a big deal. Called "The Marching 100", the band soon grew to well over two hundred members, and when it took the field at Wildcat football games everyone watched and listened.

Dick played the saxophone and would later take his talents in leading a small musical ensemble playing local events around Lexington. In the late 1950s and 60s, The Four Sounds, as they were called, became one of the city's most popular groups, landing gigs at all of the hot spots and country clubs. Dicks' wife, Jo, was an even more accomplished musician as she played piano in the group for years. One thing he did not lack was a great work ethic and even greater confidence in himself. He didn't let his growing up in what some Lexington blue bloods might refer to as the sticks stand in his way of pursuing opportunities.

In the beginning, Jo Hardin wasn't sure about Dick Walker and his happy-go-lucky approach to life and his cocky attitude. However, before long, she was all in and after a few months of dating they tied the knot with Jo dropping out of school and Dick finishing his masters at UK.

Growing up in Lexington and attending Lafayette High School, Jo came from a hard working mother and father. Her mother stayed at home to tend to the household, and raising Jo and her younger brother Eddie, while her father kept the phones working as an employee of South Central Bell, a job he would keep all of his life until his retirement in 1978. Before then, in 1965, the Hardin family had moved to a quaint little community just a few minutes from Lexington, called Troy.

For Jo's parents, college was never an option. "The Great Depression" put a stop to a lot of things in the 1930s, and even though her dad graduated from high school in 1932, his main concern was a roof over his head, clothes on his back, and putting food on the table. College for him was not even a second thought, but a job was.

For Bill and Hazel Hardin they wanted the best for their children, and education was the starting line for a future. With Jo able to live at home and even work part-time, the Hardins felt like she would be able to make it to college. With unemployment hovering just below twenty-five percent across the country, Jo's dad felt fortunate to have a good paying job as a telephone pole climber with BellSouth. Maybe, just maybe, his kids would have a chance at something he and Hazel never had.

For Dick and Jo, their relationship seemed headed in the right direction. With similar small town backgrounds and families knowing the value of a dollar, the two were quick to recognize bowling was not in their crystal ball. But music was.

Dick's time at UK was special. Adolph Rupp was turning out championship basketball teams while playing home games in the 11,000-seat Memorial Coliseum. However, it was the football program that Dick always claimed a connection. Paul "Bear" Bryant was beginning to build on a resume that had begun a few years earlier at the University of Maryland. Getting his Wildcat teams to a bowl game became the normal, and Dick, while a student, participated as well.

"Dad used to tell people he played for Bear Bryant in two different bowl games," Tony said. "They were impressed, and he never told them he played in the marching band, not on the football team."

Those band performances he was talking about were in front of 82,000 fans at the Sugar Bowl in New Orleans in 1951, and 75,000 fans at the 1952 Cotton Bowl in Dallas.

While tuition was $600, room and board $690, and books another $50, by today's standards it was seemingly affordable. But, also keep in mind the average salary for a man in 1951 was $4,700, and a woman $3,300. At the time a new car cost $2,000 and a nice house could be purchased for $7,500. For sure times were different, and so were finances, in a big way.

Dick Walker, who went by Richard in several of his band photos at UK, never seemed out of place in a school that had a reputation for drawing kids from small towns. Never short on confidence in himself nor in his ability to try something new, combined with his good looks, he was right at home in Lexington at the University of Kentucky. It mattered little that the university had more than twice the number of students as his hometown of Drakesboro had population.

Following Dick's graduation in 1955, he and Jo were married in 1956. He was in graduate school, finishing up a social studies degree that he hoped would land him a good job. Jo and Dick would soon marry and in 1957 their first son, Marty was born. Three years later son Tony arrived.

Dick made the most of his college degree. Working as a social worker and serving as the executive director of a children's home in Lexington, the couple had the means to purchase a small brick home. Built shortly after WWII, it was considered a middle class home in a blue-blood city. By now, Dick and Jo had their second son Tony, and the three bedroom and single bath home with a detached garage seemed to be enough. After all was said and done, it was a step up from what they had grown up with back in Drakesboro and Lexington. Their future looked bright. Each of the boys had a bedroom, a garage for their car, and so what if they had just one bathroom to share. That was common in the '60s.

Dick was bringing home a paycheck, and Jo was able to stay at home and take care of Marty and Tony. And besides, both thought they could make a little extra by putting their musical talents to use.

With Dick being considered one of the best saxophone players in town and Jo on the piano, they formed "group bands" that performed for parties and gatherings all over town. Make no mistake, Lexington was, and is, a party town. It seemed like high society always had something going on, so the musical thing for Dick and Jo offered steady work.

"All the horse farms had something going on and they needed music," recalled Marty Walker, Tony's older brother. "I filled in some of the time as a drummer, I was 14."

The Walkers frequented thoroughbred farms owned by Preston and Anita Madden, Leslie Combs at Spendthrift Farm, and C.V. Whitney Farm. There were several upscale hotels around as well as country clubs. They played the type of music high rollers enjoyed. Referred to as the "Keeneland Crowd," and dressed to the nines, patrons would dine and dance to easy listening sounds played by Dick and Jo Walker. The extra jobs around Lexington meant extra money for the family. However, it came with a price.

"I know my mother said later she hated leaving Marty and me with a babysitter at nights," Tony said, "and many of their gigs were on weekends."

A Master's degree in social work can take on several types of vocations, none of which are going to elevate to a top tier income. But what was going on in Dick's life was enough to make him happy. He was well-respected and doing what he could to provide for his family. It was his generation for the most part that had begun to earn more than their parents. His dad Harry and mother Anita always tried to do their best to improve their situation. Harry had actually worked for the local mining operation's company store before opening his own general store in Drakesboro.

Dick's education at UK had prepared him well, and graduate school had allowed him to fill in as a teacher in several classes his last couple of years. It also helped financially with his new family.

He had been educated, and to a certain degree trained in dealing with individuals, families, and couples, who were having difficult situations in their lives. It could be and sometimes was stressful dealing with other people's problems, and it was common for social workers to have their job affect their own family relations. Occasionally a social worker would say, "We can solve everybody's problem but our own."

For many in this profession the main issue would involve children, and Dick got a firsthand view of this when he became the director of a children's home in Lexington.

For Tony and older brother Marty their childhood revolved around sports. Lots of backyard games of all kinds, but it was baseball that soon took center stage in their young lives. They could play, just the two of them, throwing a baseball back and forth. And before long the two were pitching and catching for the Tom's Roasted Peanut Cubs, a little league team in the southern part of Lexington.

"Tony was a much better athlete than me," Marty said. "He was a phenom. To make the little league in Lexington as a nine-year-old was a big deal. There he was at that age striking out twelve year-olds."

Their dad had found time to play some fast-pitch softball, coach church league softball, and was proud of his two boys' success when they won their little league city championship.

"The competition back then was really tough," recalled Tony. "I remember as a nine-year-old, pitching against the likes of Dom Fucci and his brother Bo. They were really good. Billy and Bobby Knight, who played on the Rebels were, too. There was also Jeff

Parrot, who was a teammate of mine on the Cubs. He made it to the major leagues."

Dom Fucci became a basketball and baseball star at Tates Creek High School, where in 1975 he was Kentucky's Mr. Basketball. He later played both sports at Auburn University.

Chapter Three
"EVEN IF YOU'RE DEAD BROKE, ACT LIKE YOU'VE GOT ENOUGH MONEY TO BUY THE PLACE."

The Walker family was on the verge of experiencing something that none of them had gone through before . . . divorce.

Even though it was a topic Dick had talked and counseled others about, now it was happening to him and his family.

It was 1970, and before long Dick had moved out of their home to a small basement apartment in Lexington. Marty was thirteen years-old and Tony ten. Still, they did the best they could to retain the basics of a family.

Their mother, Jo, was a strong lady, committed to what was best for Tony and Marty. Other than the boys, it had been their music that kept them bonded, but now that seemed to be going by the wayside, too. With Jo dropping out of college for the marriage, and without the education she had sought earlier, she was compelled to look for work outside the home. Dick's meager salary was just enough to sustain him, and what he gave to Jo to help with the kids wasn't enough to lead a quality life in Lexington.

Jo found work as a clerical assistant with an insurance company. It was nine-to-five making minimum wage. For sure she had her hands full taking care of the household, two high energy boys, and worrying about if she would have enough money to make it all work. Her meager salary of $1.45 per hour and the alimony she received from Dick was it.

It had never been easy street for Dick and Jo, even from the beginning. Dick's income was such that, like many middle-class families of the time, they lived pay-check-to-pay-check. That's why their music gigs had become almost a necessity for them. Money had always been an issue. Managing money was not one of Dick's strongest traits, and as Tony remembers it, led to much of the problems in their marriage.

Tony, like a lot of kids growing up in a divorced family, has memories, especially when he and Marty would go out when visiting their dad. But there was one in particular that has stayed with him through the years.

"Following the divorce from mom, dad did his best to stay connected with us. One of my favorite places to go was to a golf place in Lexington, located on Mason Headley Road. It had a putt-putt, driving range and a par three eighteen-hole course. This is where the three of us went," says Tony. "Keep in mind dad had very little money. He was renting a basement apartment and paying alimony. We were going to do it all, putt-putt, share a bucket of range balls and believe it or not, dad sprang for a sleeve of very expensive golf balls so each of us would have a new one."

As Tony tells the story, Marty, hitting first off the tee, launched his ball over the high fence that was supposed to keep it from landing on the nearby driving range. Now, down to two golf balls, their dad directed Marty to hit another one. This time Marty's second shot was worse than the first.

"We only had one ball left for the three of us, and we were just on the first tee," Tony continued. "Dad was furious. So, when he said, 'Tony, it's your turn,' you can imagine the pressure I felt. Luckily, I hit it in front of the green."

Tony says he didn't know how they were going to keep playing with just one ball between the three of them.

"Suddenly dad said, 'Hey boys pick up some of those range balls in the fairway and put 'em in your pockets.'"

Problem solved.

"Tons of balls had been hit from the driving range onto the first fairway, so we were ready to play the rest of the holes."

Suddenly, a small Jeep-like vehicle with a driver sitting in a cage came sliding up next to the green.

"He was a big guy, a John Candy look-alike. My dad, acting like he had just seen him, sarcastically said, 'Whatcha need, Tiger?'"

The Jeep driver asked if they had any range balls. With Tony's and Marty's pockets bulging with range balls, Dick Walker, as only he could do said, "Man, what would we want with a bunch of range balls . . . we got enough money to buy this place."

After dad said that he looked down and putted, Tony added.

By Tony's admission and the purpose of retelling this story about Marty and his dad, the three of them together, it was a reminder that it doesn't take a lot of money to build memories.

"I have a smile on my face whenever I tell that story," he says. "It was one of those rare moments with dad when his care-free attitude toward money became a memory."

Tony and Marty still talk about that day in a good way. Being part of their dad's on-the-fly quickly manufactured story was worth more than a lot of money in the bank.

As busy as Dick and Jo were, they still found time to be involved with their boys. Both were active in school, and during the summer they all turned their attention to sports.

Dick coached church league sports, and also served as the assistant coach to Dr. Don Herren, at that time the minister at Southern Hills Methodist Church, located just a few hundred yards from the little league field where Tony and Marty played. Dr. Herren had become well known in the Lexington area for his success as a little league coach. Tony and Marty still to this day talk about the fun they had playing under coach Herren.

Dick and Jo were typical of most middle class couples with children in Lexington, Kentucky, during those times.

Still, Dick seemed to be trying to improve his financial situation. Once he and Jo divorced, their musical jobs dried up, at least together. For a while he managed small gigs here and there, and professionally he oversaw Kentucky Village, a juvenile detention center in Lexington, before heading up the Children's Bureau, a children's advocacy organization.

For Jo Walker, as difficult as it was financially following their divorce and being considered one of the best at playing ballads on piano, she landed a job playing at the upscale Lafayette Club in downtown Lexington. It was an 800-members-only exclusive lunch and dinner venue that opened in 1974, in the newly completed Chase Building. Past guests had included President Gerald Ford, House Speaker Tip O'Neill, and TV newsman Charles Kuralt. Located on the fourteenth floor, it offered the premier view of downtown Lexington. However, by late December 2007, membership had fallen off to 300 and the club soon closed its doors.

Tony's granddad had retired from BellSouth in 1978 after forty-three years. He was sixty-five. Little did he or Tony know then that his retirement would, years later, become the central theme of Tony's story as he developed a successful financial business.

The pension money that Bill Hardin received arrived every month like clockwork. To this day, Tony still recalls his granddad pulling up to the mailbox and grabbing out that check. His employer referred to that monthly guaranteed retirement check as a pension. Tony's granddad called it Mailbox Money®, and it was granddad's to live on the rest of his life.

Tony had seen what had happened to both sets of his grandparents. Dick's parents had no safety net when they quit working. Operating his grocery store in Drakesboro to support his family did not provide a retirement pension, so he was living paycheck to paycheck. And that's all Dick knew. That's the influence he grew up with.

On the other hand, Jo's parents knew that someday Bill would retire, and along with his social security check, would be able to continue the modest lifestyle he and wife Hazel were living. Not only was money coming in, but for the most part Bill and Hazel were worry free. That is another theme Tony has used in his presentations over the years . . . The WorryFree Retirement®.

Tony's granddad was able to tinker with all his inventions, in which he even patented a couple, watch TV, and not worry about anything.

Even as a youngster, Tony was very much aware of his surroundings, and always observant. Not only had he kept an eye on granddad's Mailbox Money®, but he was keenly attuned to all of the tinkering here and there that he had done with machinery. He could do and fix just about anything.

It seemed to be a part of a family tradition when Tony enrolled in an automobile mechanic class his sophomore year at Bowling Green High School. He had just received the black 1962 VW Beetle as a birthday gift on his sixteenth birthday from his grandparents. Knowing what engine problems that a stick shift car could encounter that was almost as old as Tony, it made good sense that he learned how to work on it himself.

"It really worked out good for me," said Tony. "While in shop class, I worked on that car all the time as part of my class. It was part of my curriculum. The car's top speed was 55 mph, and I remember going back and forth from Bowling Green to Lexington. Back in 1976, highway speed limits were set at 55 miles per hour, so I just fell in with everybody else.

"VW's were very popular back then, and as a high school student, my shop teacher, Charlie Glass, boasted to all of the faculty who would bring their VW's to me to work on, that I was "Bowling Green High School's Volkswagen specialist". He was really proud of that. I will always appreciate the way Mr. Glass treated me and made me feel like I actually was a good VW mechanic," says Tony.

Chapter Four
"NEVER ASSUME ANYTHING; THINGS CAN CHANGE IN A HEARTBEAT."

There came a day in 1973, when Dick Walker had an opportunity to improve his professional position when a job offer came his way. There was only one big issue. The job was out of town. It would mean leaving a town he had been living in for almost a quarter of a century, and it would also mean leaving his two teenage sons.

By now Dick had re-married, and he and his new wife moved to Bowling Green where he became the executive director of Region IV Barren River Mental Health, and as a licensed social worker he was responsible for a ten-county area. It was a big job with big responsibilities. It was also a transition that at the time was the beginning of life changing events for Tony.

Two years later, in 1975, Tony and his mother decided it might be better if he moved to Bowling Green with his dad.

The decision was not easy. Like many teenagers, there often were parental issues and they all felt like the move would be good for the family. Still, Tony, all his life had been very close to his older brother, Marty, and leaving him and his mother wasn't easy.

"I tagged along with Marty everywhere he went," says Tony. "I played with older kids all of my life. So I knew I would miss Marty and my mom."

The summers were spent back in Lexington where Tony enjoyed seeing his old friends, hanging out with Marty, and picking up work in restaurants washing dishes and bussing tables.

When the school year began Tony enrolled as a sophomore at Bowling Green High School. Immediately, he wanted to play on the varsity football team. And while he had played many a sandlot games with his brother and his older friends, Tony had only played one year of organized football as the quarterback his freshman year at Southern Junior in Lexington. Still, never lacking confidence in anything he did, he made the team at Bowling Green High School and as a sophomore returned kicks.

"I got my growth early," he recalled. "As I got older the other kids caught up with me. I wanted to play quarterback, of course."

Tony was always fast, and football was a sport that could take advantage of his speed. Besides playing quarterback for Southern Junior, Tony was also the punter and the starting free safety. With an undefeated season going, Southern Junior was riding high with an undefeated season until the fourth game against Jesse Clark Junior High, when Tony broke his collarbone while trying to tackle a hard-nosed running back. After the loss of Tony, Southern went on to lose their next three games.

The following year as a sophomore at Bowling Green High, playing under Coach Wilson Sears, Tony was the designated kickoff and punt return man.

"Football was my sport early on," he said. "I was excited about the season. Our first game was against Hopkinsville. On the first punt of the game, I fumbled, and they recovered. I will never forget that incident, and it made me all the more determined to never fumble the ball again."

Athletics seemed to come easy for Tony and when basketball season rolled around, he made the Purples squad.

Bob Hoggard was considered one of the best high school basketball coaches in Kentucky. In 26-years of coaching he amassed a 542-248 record and took three different teams to the Sweet 16: Christian County, Oldham County and Bowling Green. It was the Bowling Green team that Tony was a part of and by his senior season, he was the starting point guard. However, that same year a verbal altercation with Coach Hoggard quickly led to his dismissal from the team. That was the same year the Purples would make the Sweet 16, without the need of Tony's services as point guard.

"The incident with Coach Hoggard taught me a valuable lesson about life and served as a reminder as to who was in charge and keeping one's mouth shut. It also reminded me that the show will go on, with or without me," Tony said.

That year the Bowling Green team had talent. With stars George Nichols, Felton Ray, Danny Corothers, Brad Whitlow, and Rayford Brown, they defeated Maysville before losing to Covington Holmes in the quarterfinals. Their final record was 27-6.

Although Tony played all three sports his sophomore year, baseball was his best sport. As a nine-year-old kid humming fast balls past twelve-year-olds, Tony was something special. In an article that appeared in the *Lexington Leader*, Tony's coach, Don Herren, referred to Tony as the next Rick Derrickson, a former little league standout at Southern Little League that would go on to pitch in the pros. Because of his speed, and his ability to get on base, he was a base-stealing threat every time. Playing as the starting shortstop his sophomore, junior, and senior years at Bowling Green High School, he was part of teams coached by Clarence Thomas and then Steve Long. Over that three-year span, Tony would steal 121 bases while only thrown out twice. As for his skills at shortstop, Coach Long commented that he was one of the best to ever play the position at Bowling Green High.

"We were pretty good," Tony recalled. "We took spring trips to Florida and held our own with just about everybody we played. We were loaded. Our team included Jim Pickens, Jr., Mark Stahl, Monty Holland, Steve Thornton, Mike Boggs, Doug Beard, Kenny Reynolds, Joe Roberts, and Bobby Currens."

Years later, Jim Pickens had great memories of his high school days as Tony's teammate.

"He had already played against good competition by the time he moved to Bowling Green," he recalled. "I first met Tony playing against him in the Babe Ruth League, and then in high school we became a pretty good double-play combo with him at short stop and me at second base. We had great chemistry... didn't need to say a word."

Pointing to Tony's leadership on the team, even at a young age, Pickens says it was his speed that set him apart from everyone else on the team.

"He could run like a deer," said Pickens, an accomplished, award-winning sportswriter for several decades. "He was our leadoff hitter and most of the time he was on base, and most of the time he stole second. He stole fifty-seven bases in thirty-four games one year."

Not to be overlooked or lost on Tony's athletic abilities was his membership in the National Honor Society at Bowling Green High School.

"There were several subjects I intentionally avoided," he said. "Chemistry, biology, and technology were a few. I would not have made a good doctor."

The Purples went to the state tournament in 1976 and 1978, Tony's sophomore and senior years. One year of American Legion baseball, with Coach Long as his coach, Tony thought might better prepare him for college ball.

"I got a letter from Coach Tuffy Horne at UK," said Tony. "He came to Bowling Green to watch me play and made me an offer to walk-on at UK. He wanted me to play there. But, right after my senior year, UK had a coaching change and Keith Madison took over. I had to try out for UK's baseball team and assumed I was a shoo-in to make it, but instead was cut from the team during tryouts." Another lesson learned from sports, "Never assume anything."

Tony attended the University of Kentucky his freshman, sophomore, and junior years. In the meantime, he continued a long-distance relationship with his high school sweetheart, Susan Moore.

"It was mostly by letter," he said. "While we did talk some by phone, because of the high cost of long-distance calls, we couldn't afford to talk a lot. It was tough maintaining a long-distance relationship. I am so grateful Susan and I were able to hold it together."

Susan was in college at Western Kentucky University (WKU) preparing for a future in nursing. Tony was still undecided as to what his major was going to be, although he had taken several psychology classes. Thinking he could follow in the footsteps of his father and become a social worker, those classes were something to fall back on if nothing else came his way.

Once again, Tony was ready to make a move that would turn out to be in his best interest, and help prepare for his future. Up until then it had been a future full of uncertainties. The only thing he was sure of, however, was that he wanted Susan Moore to be in any future he had.

Enrolling at Western Kentucky University in 1981, Tony moved back to Bowling Green, deciding on a double major in broadcast journalism and psychology. Western Kentucky University was highly respected in the field of broadcasting, with many of its graduates landing high profile jobs. After all, Tony had always been good at speaking and never seemed at a loss for words. His grandmother Walker used to say that, "Tony had high verbal needs." Broadcasting was what he wanted to do. It fit nicely with his natural talent of being comfortable speaking his mind to others.

Since Tony was on the "five-year plan" in college, he decided it wouldn't hurt to also major in psychology as a backup in case the broadcast thing didn't work out. After all, his dad had had a successful career in the field and Tony's older brother, Marty, was following the social worker path that he was familiar with.

At first Tony lived with his dad before moving into a small cottage in Bowling Green. Having his own space would be good for everybody. And he knew at some point he would have to get a job.

Marty Walker did, in fact, give Bowling Green and Western a try, living with Tony and his dad for two years. But, in the end he was a Lexington guy. A well-known drummer there, he was able to play his way through college performing at the Campbell House, Fireplace, and Chevy Chase Inn. While now retired from the social working business, Marty still plays in a band in Lexington to this day.

Even as a youngster, Tony never ventured far from his values of growing up always having to work. That part he never wavered from, realizing that if he was going to make it in life, it would be up to him.

He dug deep, bringing with him an "I'm-gonna-do-it" attitude that he would soon draw on to keep him going. In looking back to his teenage years, he even found something positive in the divorce of his parents.

"Their divorce actually made me stronger, allowing me to experience things I wouldn't have if they had stayed married. I always remind my three kids that if my parents had never divorced, I would have never met your mother and you would have never been born. I guess I have just always tried to see the good in what others might see as the bad."

During the summers Tony worked wherever he could find a job, washing dishes at a restaurant, cooking fried chicken, and even burying telephone cable. But, in the summer of 1981, it was a college friend who tipped him off that there might be something better out there.

"He was running his own painting business and encouraged me to start my own," Tony said. "What did I know about painting houses? Nothing."

Of course, that didn't stop him. He figured it beat all of the odd jobs he'd been doing, and for sure the financial rewards would be greater.

Collegiate Painting Services was born.

The twenty-year-old college kid borrowed a twenty-eight-foot extension ladder from Granddad Hardin, bought a few paintbrushes and drop cloths, put on his "painter whites," familiarized himself with some of the Bowling Green paint stores, and was off and running. He did it with a confidence he was born with, being the son of Dick Walker, you know, the former bowling instructor. Soon he was getting contractor's prices on everything he bought.

In the beginning business came slowly. He personally delivered flyers to residents around Bowling Green that simply read, "Help a kid through college, let me paint your house." It worked. People called and soon referrals led to more business.

Tony's ability to talk to people, his work ethic and attention to detail, along with his pleasant personality, allowed him to get all the painting jobs he could handle. Word spread quickly about this young kid who showed up on time to paint their house . . . and did it right.

For three summers Tony painted houses. For a young man it was a great entrepreneur start-up. It required very little investment to get going, and although it was not always easy, he enjoyed doing it. Before long he earned enough money to buy Susan an engagement ring.

Sailing through the required curriculum for his degree in 1983, his life seemed to be in order. Not only was he armed with a college diploma, but more importantly a wedding date had been set for his marriage to Susan. Yes, 1983 would be a big year.

By Tony's own admission, he was in no-man's land when it came to religion during that period of his life. While raised in church as a youngster, Tony had drifted far from it now. His future bride, Susan, was raised Catholic and was entrenched in her church's faith. When told by Susan's priest that Tony would have to be married in a Catholic Church, Tony, had no problem being a part of the necessary requirements to receive the sacraments of holy matrimony. All he knew was that he wanted Susan to be his wife.

Tony and Susan were married August 20, 1983, in Holy Spirit Catholic Church in Bowling Green. Marty, Tony's brother, served as his best man while Annette Henry was Susan's maid of honor. That same day the couple headed out for Hilton Head to honeymoon.

"My current car at the time didn't have air, so we borrowed my step-mom's car, which was a more comfortable car with air," recalled Tony.

Tony Walker, always with an abundance of confidence in everything he attempted, however, was not prepared for the rejections that came his way while looking for employment in the broadcast field.

"In 1983, with a double major from WKU, I couldn't find work," he said. "It was the biggest disappointment I'd ever had, except for getting cut from the baseball team at UK. The only offer I had was from a station in Grand Junction, Colorado, who offered me a news anchor job on weekends. I realized at that time I was just not committed to climbing the ladder of the broadcast world."

The uncertainties in his life suddenly took on a whole different importance. Now married, he and Susan had some decisions to make. Susan had just received her B.S. in nursing school at Western Kentucky University, with all kinds of job opportunities on her horizon.

It wasn't that Tony didn't have experience behind the mic or in front of the camera. There had been times when he had been thrown in the fire that taught him valuable lessons and gave him stories to tell later in life.

One of those was as a college student. He saw a bulletin board posting looking for someone to write news and spin records at a little 250-watt radio station in Franklin, Kentucky, only a few miles south of Bowling Green near the Tennessee line.

It certainly wasn't the type of job Tony envisioned he would someday have, but it would be a start if he was hired. He immediately got in touch with WFKN radio station's owner Henry Stone. Stone was a no-nonsense, get-to-the-point radio journalist, a longtime veteran in the business. When it came to small town radio,

Stone was a legend in the business across Kentucky. One of his claims to fame came in 1968, when Johnny Cash and June Carter slipped out of Tennessee to get married in Franklin, Kentucky. One of Cash's friends had heard of Stone, and on that first day of March asked if he would tape record the wedding ceremony. Stone set his reel-to-reel recorder up and stood just off to the side as the two country music stars said their vows.

Tony was smart enough to know that he could learn a lot if he got the job. In typical Henry Stone style, the interview didn't last long. He saw and heard enough from Tony to know he was his man.

"I was hired on the spot," said Tony. "I was going to handle any news that came in on Saturdays and Sundays, plus had to open up the station on Sunday mornings at 5:30 a.m. so I could put on the preachers and gospel singers."

Sunday morning at small town radio stations are big across Kentucky, and the little station in Franklin was no different.

"He told me that's when all the preachers and gospel singers come to the studio and sing live on the air," Tony said. "Like clockwork, on each half-hour, a new preacher or gospel singer would stroll into the radio station and hand me twenty bucks for thirty minutes. They would proceed into a separate studio, and I'd flip on their mic and off they would go for the next thirty minutes while I sat and read the newspaper or studied for my next college exam."

When they were gone, Tony had some time on his hands as he played records and talked. Not knowing how many, if any, were listening to the station at 5:30 in the morning, he had a little fun by developing some character voices on the air.

"I came up with an Elwood P. Goldrush character," he said. "It was fun. I've used those voices along the way. My dad used to listen to me on the radio and always got a good laugh when I'd take on Elwood . . . Susan, not so much!"

For eighteen months Tony did this every Saturday and Sunday. Finally, he realized the importance of what was taking place. Not only had he learned from Henry Stone how to construct a good news story, but also the role of a little radio station and what it meant to a community.

Chapter Five
"DON'T LOOK A GIFT HORSE IN THE MOUTH... WHEN OPPORTUNITY PRESENTS ITSELF, JUMP ON IT."

Now at the age of twenty-three, and knowing his only serious job offer was in Colorado, Tony applied to a multitude of TV stations. With lots of confidence, he knew he was good enough to be an on-air reporter or sportscaster. He even tried locally, but only to find no one was looking for a young sportscaster.

Tony, still searching, wanted to stay in Bowling Green. That's where Susan grew up and it was where her parents, Bill and Della Moore were well established in the community. Bill owned one of the top insurance agencies, and Della taught school at Parker Bennett Elementary.

Being an insurance agent was something that never crossed Tony's mind. After all, he knew where he wanted to go and what he wanted to do, but the problem was getting there.

Finally, realizing he needed to make some decent money, he took a sales position with a local radio station. Rick Williams, a career radio executive, was the sales manager of that station in 1983, when Tony went to work there.

"You could tell Tony was determined to be successful, even back then," said Williams. "He was eager to learn and really believed in himself. He knew, however, he wanted more than selling radio advertising."

For the first time in his life he was second guessing himself. His education in broadcast journalism and psychology seemed of little value at this point in his life. Thank goodness for Susan and the security of the good nursing job she had.

Tony and Susan were very happy with each other, but not so much with where Tony was in building a future. Susan's parents could see the stress, too.

"We had been to dinner with her parents," Tony said. "We were driving home and sitting in the back seat when suddenly Mr. Moore looks in the rearview mirror and asks, 'Tony how'd you like to be in the insurance business?'" It was 1984, and Tony Walker's world was about to change again.

Bill Moore bought his insurance agency several years earlier from Chester Hock and had grown the property casualty business into one of the largest in Bowling Green. Physically, Moore had overcome polio as a youngster, but not enough to have to give up a baseball scholarship to Notre Dame. A graduate of St. Joe High School in Bardstown, he was determined and able to earn his degree from the school in South Bend.

By the way, Bill's older brother was General Hal Moore, portrayed by actor Mel Gibson in the movie "We Were Soldiers."

Now earning $11,700 a year at his new job, Tony occupied a small cubicle near the front door of the State Street office of Bill Moore Insurance.

A lot had happened in Tony's life in the last year and a half—college graduate, marriage, and now working for his father-in-law. He wasn't complaining by any means. In fact, he felt fortunate to be where he was. Now, he and Susan had jobs they could count on.

Don't think for a minute, however, that Tony was on easy street because of Susan's dad. Far from it. Bill Moore was a task master, demanding, but fair, and in the military style of his General brother, it was full speed ahead. By now in Moore's life he was wearing braces on both legs and used a cane for assistance as a result from the polio. Still, he oversaw a successful business in which not only Tony, but another son-in-law, Jeff Hilliard and son Jim were also employed.

Tony, in spite of high interest rates at the time, and a questionable economy across the country, hit the ground running.

"My job was to get out and sell homeowners and auto insurance," he said. "I made cold calls, even selling earthquake coverage. I'd ride around Bowling Green, take Polaroid photos, and personally deliver a proposal with the picture of their home. I just knocked on doors. Most of the people were very friendly and I was well received."

Like everything Tony ever did, he was all in. His work ethic and competitive spirit along with a creativity even in the insurance business, let those around him and especially his father-in-law know how determined and driven he was to be successful.

Susan, in 1986, gave birth to their first child, Phillip, so it was one more reason Tony was motivated to be a provider for his new family.

In 1988, four years after he began with Bill Moore Insurance, Tony qualified as Charter Life Underwriter, a designation that meant he was now able to assist clients with estate planning and various levels of expertise in life insurance. He could inform clients and potential clients how much insurance was needed. At the age of twenty-nine-years-old, Tony attained one of the most respected insurance certifications in the industry.

"I was one of the youngest in the nation to reach that level," said Tony. "I really enjoyed getting people to think about their future . . . to think about things they hadn't done before."

Tony was making good money, and now the stoplight of life was turning from red to yellow to green. The insurance business was rolling, and for Tony and Susan it was about to get even better.

"Mr. Moore turned the company over to Jim, Jeff, and me," said Tony. "Everything really looked good for us at first. But then Jeff sold his portion of the business to Jim, and when that happened, I became a minority stock owner."

Tony quickly realized his position in the insurance company would not serve him well and left his future there in question. Some feathers were ruffled and Jim, Susan's brother, let it be known that perhaps the business was not big enough for them both.

"I sold out my stock to Jim with a three-year non-compete clause," Tony said. "I then opened a second-floor office on 10th Street, and called my business The Walker Group, with an emphasis on helping business owners and high-net worth individuals set up plans to reduce estate taxes upon their deaths. At that time estate tax rates affected a lot of people."

Not selling insurance, and now solely concentrating on this new field of estate planning, meant reverting back to something he became good at several years previously . . . cold calling.

Chapter Six
"HARD WORK BEATS DUMB LUCK EVERY TIME."

To this day, Tony's mother, Jo Walker, still lives in Lexington in the same house Tony and brother Marty were raised in with the same back yard that captured all of those memories of the two brothers playing pitch and catch.

In 1990, with things not going great in his new start-up company, The Walker Group, Tony and Susan had come to a fork in the road. Tough decisions had to be made. Susan had a good nursing job and had been the major bread winner for a good portion of their marriage. It wasn't that Tony wasn't trying. He always had a job, but his drive for success was not being met, at least the way he anticipated. Others would have been satisfied with what Tony had accomplished, but not him.

Bill Robbins, who was the owner of Bill Robbins Insurance in Lexington, just happened to be a high school classmate of Tony's mother at Lafayette High School. Bill shared with Jo that he could use another insurance producer in his office. When Tony's mother relayed the job opening to Tony, he jumped at the offer.

At a young age Tony had overcome several challenges, and with his CLU certification he could get his foot in the door of most insurance agencies. His non-compete clause in Bowling Green meant if insurance was his route, he would have to leave town, and Bill Robbins in Lexington maybe, just maybe, could be the answer.

"It was sort of crazy, looking back on it," said Tony. "We had a cute little house on Hill Road in Bowling Green. Sold it for $60,000, packed up, and headed to Lexington. Phillip was three-and-a-half years old."

Bill Robbins had been in business for several decades, and Tony was smart enough to surround himself with people who knew the ropes, and he could learn from them. The Robbins Agency also had in the same building a well-respected insurance producer by the name of Art Solomon who also wanted to work with Tony. He was the owner of a successful wealth planning group.

"Both Mr. Robbins and Art taught me a lot," said Tony. "I learned the value of having lots of appointments. Art Solomon was one of the hardest working men I had ever been around. I realized that if you were going to be successful in this business, you had to see a lot of people, and I was fine with that."

Living in a rented house in Lexington, and with Susan doing a few nursing jobs here and there, the young Walker family was doing the best they could to right their ship that had slightly been tipped over from his Bill Moore Insurance days, when by all appearances they had settled in for an exciting future.

Tony was doing his best. Treading water in the business world usually means you are going backwards, and for sure progress was not in his vocabulary, except for the contacts with Robbins and Solomon.

Following the birth of their second child Lacey in March 1991, with Tony floundering to make it in Lexington, in June of that same year Tony and Susan made the decision to return to Bowling Green. They had been in Lexington a little over a year.

Tony's personal finances were dire. By his own admission, he ran through much of the money he and Susan had. It wasn't that he was a spendthrift. No, it was completely the opposite. It cost money to operate a business, pay rent, and provide for a family.

"It got so bad at one point that I had to borrow money from Susan's dad," Tony said. "I'm sure the Moore's were disappointed in me for all of the turmoil in the business, and it did cause some dissension."

Still, Susan's mother and father had faith in what Tony could and would accomplish. "I'll be forever grateful that the Moores continued to have faith in me and always encouraged me to keep working hard," said Tony.

As uncertain as the years were in 1989 through 1991, inspite of the struggles financially and emotionally, Susan was still able to point to those times with good memories.

"It was one of the happiest times of my life," she said.

At thirty-one years-old, Tony had not given up on conquering the world. Although here and there his confidence in himself had seen its good and bad days, he was re-energized with his move back to Bowling Green.

In 1991, he reopened his downtown office above Checks Pool Room, space he rented from attorney Jerry Parker.

While Tony and Susan were still trying to figure it all out, another of life's obstacles began to raise its ugly head.

For some time things hadn't been quite right with Tony's dad. As the head of the area's mental health organization, he began to experience issues of his own. Soon, everyone close to Dick Walker knew the one-time-personality-plus man needed to be cared for in a nursing home. Only in his late fifties, Dick was diagnosed with Alzheimer's and died in a nursing home in 1996. He was only sixty-four. Watching his father die at such a young age taught Tony to always appreciate today because you never know what tomorrow might bring; a truism the Bible speaks to as well. Yet, just as God took one loved one from Tony's life, he brought another new life into Tony and Susan's world when in 1995, their youngest, Anthony was born.

In life it seems that everybody needs to catch a break along the way, though it wasn't that Tony was looking for something to fall out of the sky. He had, at least he thought, done everything possible to check the right boxes professionally in order to attain the professional advancements required to continue an upward spiral.

Perhaps a realignment was in order.

"Working in the past with Art Solomon taught me that I had to work harder and see more people. I realized I needed to work with more people who also had money they needed managed for their retirement," he said. "In 1995, I decided that the field of "Money Management" needed to be my direction."

Tony was on top of what was happening on Wall Street. As complicated as it seemed to be, he had a way of simplifying things. It was then that he decided his future clients would not be the super rich, but instead be those who were Savers, not Investors. Tony referred to his new-found clients as the "Joe Lunchbox" type, folks who were just like his granddad—hard-working, who didn't like risking all of their money in the stock market.

"Most Savers don't like losing a lot of money; they are not comfortable with taking a lot of risk," he pointed out. "And Wall Street doesn't understand that."

Tony made an acquaintance in Glasgow, Kentucky, that would validate the direction he was headed in as a money manager.

"It was definitely a break for me when I met Howard Gray," Tony said.

Gray headed up Gray Construction, a large company that had recently, in 1988, moved its company headquarters from rural Glasgow to downtown Lexington. The company has gone on to become global with offices throughout the United States and Japan.

Tony, all of his life had been a people person, emphasizing that if you're nice to people they will be nice back. His humility, charm and humor has served him well, whether in front of large groups or one-on-one, which was the case with Gray.

"He got to know me," says Tony. "He said to me one time when I started making my plans too complicated, 'Tony, I know a lot about hammers and nails, but not much about all this planning stuff you keep talking about . . . you need to keep this stuff simple.'"

Tony learned a valuable lesson from Howard, the same lesson learned by the late-great Will Rogers who once said, "Everybody's ignorant, only on different subjects."

Even though Tony now seemed to be pulling his business plan together, and possibly with his days of cold calling now in his rearview mirror, there was still some work to be done.

By now Walker Financial moved downstairs at their 10th Street location, previously occupied as attorney offices. With more room, upgraded software, and the latest in technology, he was now ready to implement his money management practices and add to his growing list of clients. Finally, he was no longer simply selling life insurance, but now focusing on the planning end.

Through it all Tony never lost sight of how important Susan was to their survival.

With goals now altered a bit, it was still important for the Walkers to maintain a revenue stream. Tony's business had rent and employees to pay, in addition to everything else it took to maintain a first-class operation. And at home there were three kids and a mortgage payment.

"My business was sucking up the money," Tony said. "I was still struggling, borrowing money against our home. I was mortgaged to the hilt, but Susan was still all in about our future. Like her parents, Susan always had confidence in me to make it all work."

Susan, for sure, in those days, was the breadwinner. Working a twelve-hour night shift from 7 p.m. to 7 a.m. allowed the couple to be able to count on her regular paycheck from a local hospital.

On the surface Tony's business had all of the appearances of a bright future. There was, however, a period that Tony thought then had reached a low period.

"It got so bad that I had to go to Mr. Moore and borrow $25,000 just to pay off several bills we had," said Tony. "It was embarrassing."

Being the businessman his father-in-law was, he drew up a note for the money Tony borrowed. "I was shocked that he would have me sign a note for that loan. I couldn't wait to pay that note off," recalled Tony. "I made regular payments and my business began to build, which really helped."

The relationship Tony and Susan had with each other was not only through their love for each other, but also respect.

After working the twelve hours at the hospital, Susan would come home tired. She needed rest. And with three kids waiting to see their mother, it was not always easy to get.

There was one place in the house, however, that maybe could be such a place.

Their bedroom had an extra-large closet just off of it. When the door was shut, all outside noise was muffled and the small space became an oasis of silence.

Tony and Susan made the decision that she would sleep in the closet while Tony would watch the kids until noon when he would then head to work.

In a creative sort of way that same closet became the fourth bedroom of their three-bedroom home for their son Anthony.

"We had a contractor friend to cut a window into the closet," said Tony. "Susan wanted to make sure we could get some fresh air in there, especially since it would be Anthony's room."

Still working the plan, Tony kept at it, never losing his focus on the prize . . . a successful money management business.

Chapter Seven
"IT IS TRUE; YOU REALLY CAN'T TAKE IT WITH YOU."

In business, like life, young people often lack experience and credibility, but now Tony was making advancements in both. He felt as though he was ahead of his time when it came to retirement planning. In his mind he found his niche, a profession in which he could separate himself from the others who would fall into the category of stockbrokers or money managers or even advisors. Even though when it came to what he was striving for, he may not have dotted all of the "i's," he had crossed most of the "t's."

Along the way Tony was learning, and even at a relatively young age for the business he was in, he was relying on the experience he already gained. He had been an avid reader for some time, and he talked to as many people in the money profession as he could. But, most importantly, he never quit thinking about his grandfather, and in the most simplistic way how he worked for all of those years, and once he decided to retire became the recipient of what Tony would later make a central theme to his business . . . Mailbox Money®. It seemed so elementary, yet on the other hand, complex.

Tony had figured out what Wall Street was doing a few years earlier. The people who began securing money, Tony felt, were vulnerable to what the slick pitchmen from Wall Street were telling them.

"The financial world never encourages savers to use and enjoy their money," said Tony. "They want the money to stay locked up inside their 401(k) plans. When you take it from them, they lose money. It doesn't benefit the financial world for you to use your own money."

It was here that he began to see the big picture of the financial profession he was in. It became even more clear to him that there was a distinction between Savers and Investors, and if he was going to separate himself from all of the others selling something, it would be up to him to not only tell them, but show them, what they would get in return.

Tony's thought process was never ending. He was taking his granddad's lifestyle to heart, with the primary takeaway being that no matter how long his granddad lived, he would never run out of money. He didn't need a financial advisor to figure it out. Life was much simpler then. For sure he wasn't going to put his hard-earned BellSouth money in something that had gone belly-up several years before . . . the stock market. And the infamous 401(k) plan had not come into being. It was the 401(k) that replaced pensions, thus eliminating most, if not all, Mailbox Money®.

Here was the opening Tony was looking for. Come up with his version of mailbox money and show clients they could be savers and have money coming their way for the rest of their lives.

Tony was now thinking out loud. "If clients have mailbox money coming in for the rest of their lives, it needs to mean it's income they can never outlive, which translates into a worry-free retirement."

That was it. Mailbox Money® for a worry-free retirement. Who wouldn't want that?

Wall Street, and banks, too, have done their part in convincing those that save, the one way to have enough money for retirement is to invest, and yes risk, those dollars in the stock market.

"They don't care about Mailbox Money®," Tony says. "The longer you leave it with them, the more money they make and the less you get to enjoy what you have earned."

Was he on to something? He thought so. It was the edge he was looking for. Stockpiling money for the sake of security was no longer the only option. His clients had worked hard, saved their money, and now it was time to show them how to enjoy it. In other words, spend it while you can. "It's your money" was what Tony set about to tell his clients.

In dialog with clients, before they realize it Tony quickly shows them that he can help build a bridge to their money and not a wall. What he explains to them calmly rolls off his lips, putting those across the table from him at ease.

It was coming together for Tony. Everybody in the world in some form is attached to money, some more than others. But as

Tony Walker Financial began to emerge as someone in the Bowling Green area who was helping people, hardworking people, hang on to what they have, his mission now was to get the word out. Even though his granddad died broke, he and his wife lived a great life.

Tony was now realizing that unbeknownst to him, his granddad had left quite a legacy. It was much more than the 1962 VW he gave to Tony, or the $85,000 house that sold at auction when he and Hazel had passed.

"Our goal in life is to master our money," says Tony. "The way to do this is to simplify things in such a way that you know what you have and how you're going to use it, enjoy it, and protect it without worrying about how much is going to be left when you die."

Kevin O'Leary, the billionaire Shark Tank guy, offered a similar observation when he once said, "Don't cry for money . . . it never cries for you."

Those words can be twisted in several ways to mean different things. Take Tony's granddad for instance. He never cried for money, but he did work hard climbing all of those poles for BellSouth. And in return a good retirement came back to him. So perhaps the money did cry for him.

His granddad, without knowing it, had figured it out, and in the process, mastered his money.

"Beauty is in the eyes of the beholder." This is a quote most often used to describe someone or something that is probably less attractive than someone else. Money is the same way. For those who have less than others, it can be rationalized that, "You can't take it with you." In other words, when you die that money will be left for someone else to enjoy or fight over.

In the year 1996, Tony, now only thirty-six years-old, had been in the financial business for twelve years. For the most part he had put those cold calls selling insurance in his experience memory book.

Still, Tony Walker was no way, no how, set financially for life. With three kids, and a supportive wife working twelve-hour nursing shifts, he was, it seemed, always having to borrow to make it.

Results from his hard work, long hours and a persistence and confidence he had in himself, however, was beginning to pay off.

Although Tony didn't inherent how to earn money from his own father, he did come away with charm, the ability to speak, and, above all, self-confidence. What he had naturally would be difficult to put a price on.

Tony's lower middle class upbringing in Lexington allowed him to stay connected to where he had been. Now making his own money decisions, he had different goals when it came to work, money and the future for him, Susan and his three kids.

"I realized that if I was going to make it in life, it would be up to me," he said. "The can-do spirit that God had blessed me with kept me going. I decided to try to excel at whatever I was going to do, even back in those radio ad selling days. Looking back on it, I feel my parents' divorce actually made me a stronger person. It allowed me to experience things I wouldn't have, had they stayed married. I learned at a young age that no matter how bad things might appear, with the help of God's grace, there is always a silver lining in every circumstance."

Silver linings usually mean good things, and little did Tony know, but a phone call he was about to receive could possibly change everything for him.

Chapter Eight
"IT NEVER HURTS TO ASK."

For several years, Tony had been a member of the Bowling Green Area Chamber of Commerce, even serving on several committees. He was well aware of the importance of networking and meeting new business owners coming to Bowling Green.

Rick Dubose was the Chambers Executive Vice-President with one of his responsibilities overseeing the Monthly Magazine television show on the cable. Dubose, with a history in the broadcast business, called Tony to be on the show.

Tony, using the skills he learned back in his broadcast studies at Western, impressed Dubose enough that he suggested that he should consider something on a regular basis.

"He was good, a natural," said Dubose. "Tony was very comfortable in front of the camera."

Now realizing that television might be just what he needed to get the word out on his cutting-edge ideas, as they related to helping those potential clients who were nearing retirement age, he set about with a plan.

"In 1996 I made a connection with Sheryl Morris," Tony said. "She worked with the local cable company and had experience at Western. She was good at what she did."

The local show they came up with was called "Your Money Matters," and wound up airing for seven years.

"The show actually got pretty good," recalled Tony. "Sheryl was contacted by cable TV in Louisville who wanted to run the show. It was aired there twenty or thirty times a week at no cost, and before long people began to call."

"During the late 90s my production team and I, at the cable company, had experience producing all kinds of local event programming, but little experience in producing promotional videos for the business sector in Bowling Green and Warren County," Morris said.

That was about to change.

"Tony came to us with his innovative ideas to produce TV shows that could help promote his vision, passion, and mission to educate people on how to invest in their future," she continued.

Production for the show got underway at the cable company studio in Bowling Green. It didn't take Morris long to catch Tony's excitement and enthusiasm for this new adventure.

"He was always big on ideas for the show, and we were eager to add this type of production to our resume for future revenue projects," she said.

A single show took hours of prep work on Tony's part and hours of production time, according to Morris. The show was innovative, easy to comprehend and Tony, projecting his pleasing personality, was an entertaining host of the show.

"We had fun producing it," said Morris. "I would direct the show and Chris Bratton and others were the videographers and editors."

"Your Money Matters" originated out of Bowling Green, and with Tony's vision and continuing success, his audience grew and so did his business and client base.

"It was a great partnership for both of us," added Morris. "We were able to solicit more projects like Tony's in Bowling Green and surrounding counties."

Tony Walker, the self-labeled lower middle class kid, had now seemed to overcome a lack of job offers in his college field of studies . . . broadcast journalism . . . to rise to a level of starring in his own television production.

Identifying clients had been somewhat of a slow process, but now with television, he had found a whole new platform from which to tell his story.

And he had only just begun.

Taking it a step further, Tony had aspirations of creating a reality show of sorts in 2006. Titled *The Money Missionary*®, he took the thirty-minute pilot production to a conference in Orlando to see if any of the TV production companies might show an interest.

"Not a nibble," said Tony. "None."

A few months later another door opened when Tony was traveling all over the country promoting his book, *The WorryFree Retirement*®, with the subtitle: *Ten Steps to a WorryFree Retirement*®."

On one of Tony's many business trips, he met a book publicist by the name of Helen Cook who took an interest in his recent book. After sharing a copy of the book with her, she made a call to WAVE 3 TV in Louisville. At that time, a well-known TV personality, Cindy Sullivan, was hosting a show called "WAVE Listens Live". That show proved to be the break Tony was truly seeking to take his practice to the next level.

Of course, as the guest on Wave Listens Live, the show topic and request for call-ins was all about retirement, and Tony was ready.

"I remember Cindy and I sitting at the desk on the set and her saying that hopefully we will get a phone call or two," recalls Tony. "However, much to everyone's surprise that day, the phone in the Wave 3 studios rang off the hook. After the show Cindy said it was the most calls they had ever received during a show."

Tammy McNeill, at the time, was the producer of "Wave Listens Live". It was her role to make sure guests were lined up for the show with Cindy Sullivan.

"I first met Tony Walker when his publicist sent me his first book, *The WorryFree Retirement®*," recalled McNeill. "The book's content was great, and I booked him for an interview."

The 10 a.m. television show had a large listening audience, and surprisingly to McNeill, they were very interested in planning for their retirement.

Soon Tony was appearing on WAVE 3 on a semi-regular basis. By now the evolution of Tony Walker on TV was taking place. Although he might have envisioned himself sitting behind a desk reading news or sports at a major market TV station somewhere in America, here he was talking about what many Americans wanted to hear . . . their finances.

Early on, Tony had one segment of the hour-long show, but that, too, was getting ready to change.

"Shortly after, his segment became the entire show," said McNeill. "Viewers were calling asking Tony questions about their retirement and for advice."

The show was so popular that a few years later Tony had his own show every Monday on WAVE, called "The WorryFree Retirement®".

McNeill pointed out that the phone lines were full for every show.

"They liked Tony's down to earth personality and likability," she continued. "He answered each question fully, and really didn't expect the viewer to sign up for his services."

But, they did.

They trusted Tony, and often some of the viewers called in during the show and provided testimonies on how Tony had saved them money and helped them retire "worry free."

It didn't take Tony long to realize he was on to something big.

"I said, why don't you let me pay you to be on the air?" "It didn't hurt to at least ask. All they could do is say no. They had never done this before."

Never lacking the will to build his financial business, soon Tony and WAVE agreed to a one-year contract where Tony would appear as the resident retirement specialist each and every Monday. The show with Tony as the featured guest lasted from 2007 to 2014.

Tony Walker Financial was on fire.

"This really propelled my business." "It was the best money I ever spent," said Tony. "I will always be grateful for WAVE 3 giving me the opportunity to be on their show for that long."

With Louisville's market taking off, Tony began hosting workshops dealing with retirement and how clients could put their minds at ease by utilizing his formulas and ideas. Not having an office in Louisville and still making all of his appointment scheduling out of the Bowling Green headquarters, didn't slow Tony down, at least for the time being.

A staff of two in Bowling Green—Connie Fortney and Heather Hughes—were doing all they could just to keep up. Tony was meeting people in their homes, in hotel lobbies, and in coffee shops. And in a creative way he established a relationship with a Starbucks coffee shop as a regular meeting place at the corner of Shelbyville and Hurstbourne Pkwy. in Louisville.

"I paid Starbucks fifty bucks a day to meet there," he said. "In exchange for the fifty dollars, the manager gave me a gift card to use at Starbucks. The way I had it figured, I had a nice lobby, and free coffee for my clients and a lobby for prospective clients to drink coffee while they waited for their appointment. Like so many people in my life, I will always be grateful to the employees at that Starbucks who took good care of me. I would meet two days a week with clients, all day long for more than five years at that Starbucks location."

Never one to shy away from work, or in this case the opportunity to grow his business, he recognized he was spreading himself too thin. Driving 30,000 miles a year between Louisville and Bowling Green, Tony had a decision to make.

Chapter Nine
"IF YOU WANT SOMETHING INCREDIBLE, FIND OTHERS WITH THE ABILITY TO MAKE IT HAPPEN."

Tony knew what he had to do. Delegate. Susan, his wife, saw what was going on. Tony was meeting with thirty or more clients a week in Bowling Green and Louisville, and the pace at which he was going would soon suck the enthusiasm and passion out of him unless he found a solution.

"I had to come up with a process that would work," he said. "I knew it would take additional staff."

Not just any staff, though.

He needed people who were detail oriented, people who could follow up with what he started. Personalities were important. After all, his new employees would be dealing with clients that Tony had nurtured and persuaded to trust Tony Walker Financial with protecting their money. Whoever Tony brought into the business would become an extension of himself.

"I'm the idea guy," he says. "I knew if the company was to grow, I needed help. But it had to be the right people.

"To grow, and we were growing, some people think when you are successful you can slow down. Not me. This is when you need to work harder and invest more in yourself and the company."

With Tony Walker Financial growing like never before, suddenly others in the financial business began to also take notice. They had seen this so-called "new kid on the block" inch his way into what they once considered their territory.

This was particularly evident in Louisville where his TV shows had netted positive results for him from the first time it aired on WAVE Listens.

In 2014, at the age of fifty-four, Tony Walker, armed with more than thirty years in the business and a wall full of credentials, was now ready, willing, and able to take his company to another level.

Now seeing the fruits of his long hours, trips between Louisville and Bowling Green, success was beginning to emerge.

He remembered what his father-in-law, Susan's dad, told him several years earlier. "Tony," he said, "remain independent and don't be beholden to any one company or institution. You work for the customer, not the company."

But most of all, Tony kept at the forefront of his thoughts just how important and supportive Susan had been through it all. Never second guessing his ability to transfer his vision into reality, she had been there with him, bringing home paychecks from her nursing duties.

Much of Tony's drive is a result of what he experienced back in 1991, when it seemed like the bottom had fallen out for him financially.

"I had fallen into the depths of despair with no one, including Susan, having a clue of how depressed I was over the failure I felt in letting down my family by not being able to provide for them," he said. "We had no money except what she was bringing home."

It was June of that same year when spiritually Tony realized he needed help, not physical or mental help, but assistance from above.

"I was floundering, and my life was pretty low until God stepped in," he said. "What was interesting is that God was putting people in my life that were mentoring to me in ways I couldn't comprehend until God entered the picture." "It proved to me that God truly never will forsake you, no matter what you might be going through if you simply believe in him."

Growing up, Tony, brother Marty, and their parents went to church in Lexington like a lot of families. However, admittingly, he says religion had been observed at an arms length. In 1991, after he and Susan moved back to Bowling Green, a life altering thing happened.

"I became a Christian and shortly thereafter, Susan and I joined Living Hope Baptist Church," he said. "I had a lot going on in my life, and in my faith I was able to find a peace that enabled me to rethink where I was with it all." "Even in my work, although I was in the money business, my life was no longer about the money, but about serving God the best I could."

In 1993, Tony Walker had an idea. He has had them before. Lots of them, but this one was different. It had nothing to do with anything financial, but this time had to do with everything spiritual.

It all started with an invite from one of those Christian friends that was in Tony's life at that time. Mike Pressley invited Tony to attend a men's prayer breakfast in Nashville with the featured speaker being the grandson of the Adolph Coors. After hearing Mr. Coors share his testimony about how God saved him, Tony approached him and asked if he would come to Bowling Green to speak. Mr. Coors then asked Tony, "How are you going to get people there?"

With not knowing what to do or how to go about arranging a prayer breakfast, Mr. Coors suggested a prayer breakfast specialist by the name of Kermit Sutherland from California. Mr. Sutherland suggested Tony seek the help of his mayor. It just happened to be a client of Tony's by the name of Johnny Webb of Bowling Green. Tony and then Mayor Webb put their heads together and proposed the first Bowling Green Prayer breakfast.

The first event in 1993, drew over 400 business leaders to the Greenwood Executive Inn. The event would soon outgrow that location and move to the Sloan Convention Center, where over 600 people attended to hear the testimony of other business leaders and how God had affected their lives.

Mayor Webb, who at the time was just getting his feet wet in running the city, knew he wouldn't be able to pull it together by himself.

"Tony said, don't worry about it. I'll handle it, and he did," said Webb.

"I knew nothing about putting on a prayer breakfast and certainly did not have the clout with the business community to persuade them to attend such a breakfast," said Tony. "It was the influence of Johnny who made this event possible." "If not for Johnny Webb it would not have taken off," Tony recalled.

The prayer breakfast, says Tony, was to inspire and encourage the Bowling Green professional and business community, and bring them closer together in God's name.

After Webb left office, Mayor Eldon Renaud was equally supportive of the event. Tony continued to serve as the breakfasts' coordinator for eleven straight years before passing off the reigns to other area leaders.

Since June of 1991, Tony has made his spiritual relationship a part of his TV show, sprinkling Bible verses interestingly throughout, and whenever possible, what it says about money. He has never forgotten where he was within himself, and will never forget who ultimately gets all the credit for his success — God.

Tony had another decision to make. The competition was now saying Tony Walker didn't have a real presence in Louisville, that he was just an out-of-towner coming in and taking money.

He had thought for some time about opening a Louisville office, but now such talk made it an easy decision. In those days of traveling back and forth from Bowling Green to Louisville, Tony was willing to meet folks at their convenience, whether it was meeting them at their homes, in hotel lobbies, or coffee shops. It didn't matter as long as Tony was helping Savers. But all of this would soon be a thing of the past. It wouldn't be easy coming up with the perfect location as he had dealt with such a problem in Bowling Green a few years earlier when he made the decision to move from downtown to something a little further out.

Tony needed a location in Louisville that was easy to find as many of his clients were driving long distances to meet with him. In 2017, Tony lucked out and found the perfect spot at 8303 Shelbyville Road, just minutes from Oxmoor Mall, a location that would be easy for anyone to find. With a vision for a building that would meet his growing clientele, but also house his production studio, Tony purchased the building, and the rest is history. Now Tony had secured two buildings, one in Bowling Green and the other in Louisville to meet his clients.

"Prior to the purchase of the Shelbyville Road location, we had been producing the TV show in what we called the Broom closet studio in our previous location," said Aaron Orrender, the TV producer.

About this time, Tony needed an office manager in Louisville, someone who could not only keep things organized, but also a person who could oversee the placement of advertising as well as digital media and event planning. That person is Gina Tutwiler. Her background of twenty-three years at iHeartMedia made her an easy choice. "Not only does Gina run the Louisville office, but she does all of the media buying for the many TV and radio stations our weekly program airs on," said Tony. "She is one of the hardest workers in the world and truly cares about our clients, and making sure the stations we air our show on get us the best time slots available to our audience of Savers."

Chapter Ten
"NOTHING STAYS THE SAME."

Throughout Tony's life he has had flashbacks to what he recalled hearing his dad frequently say, "Nothing stays the same."

Tony may not have repeated it aloud, but he sure has replayed it in his mind. The saying has surfaced several times as Tony and Susan's life has spiraled upward since the early '90s.

So much of Tony Walker's business has resulted from his association with the right people, a willingness to read and learn, and a drive to succeed that is difficult to explain.

"It's just a drive I've always had," he simply says. "It comes from the inside, something I was born with."

Tony knew that regardless of what he personally knew or how smart he was, it was a priority to make sure his office staff was also up to the task. That's why he established a rigid criteria that includes the client always comes first. Without a client the doors don't stay open.

Tony is quick to say, "Anybody can sell you something, it's altogether another thing for someone to service what they sell." This service is why the staff, no matter what office responsibilities they have, is a top priority for Tony Walker Financial to complete their service after the sale.

Bringing the right people into Tony's team concept from the git-go remains to this day an important cog in his company's growth and success. He further realized that working conditions were a part of the overall equation.

All of this is evident with, first the expansion of his downtown office, to a move to an office center, Campus Plaza, just outside of downtown Bowling Green.

"We needed the change," he says. "We were running out of space and needed to make sure our growing staff had the room for all of us to grow the business. It also offered a more convenient place for clients to visit us."

To get to this point in Tony Walker Financial history that began in 1989 may have appeared an overnight success. Far from it. Every step of the way had become embedded in Tony and Susan's brain. All of those cold call days, meeting with clients in a second floor office downtown Bowling Green, working out of their home while meeting clients off site, and then those coffee shop and hotel lobby meetings in Louisville, they had managed to hack their way through the weeds of the business world and now see green grass.

Tony has told his clients for years, "If you are planning on retiring you've got to have a plan." But now, being the organized person he is, he had his own plan in growing Tony Walker Financial.

Connie Fortney had worked as a senior programmer analyst at Holley Performance, a high end automotive manufacturer in Bowling Green, but left in 1996 to raise her small children. A church conversation with Susan Walker led to a career change. It was 2004.

"Our office was in Campus Plaza, and I started out part-time just answering the phone," she recalled. "We had three of us in the office, but within a year-and-a-half it was just me."

All of a sudden, Fortney's role had ballooned into something much larger.

"I quickly had to learn the annuity world," she says, while recognizing that this had become a big part of Tony's plan to help Savers hang onto their money. "I was doing all of the application processing, answering the phone and doing whatever it takes to help in a busy office."

Tony's big picture plan, of course, had him becoming a fiduciary. It also included duplicating himself in order to grow the business. With Connie Fortney on board, with a take-charge personality, it would seem she would be in line to add a fiduciary title to her profile.

"Becoming a fiduciary is not my skill," she offered. "I'm an office person. I've tried to be the steady rock here to run the day-to-day business since I've been here the longest."

As Tony Walker Financial has grown, no one person has seen up close and personal to what has transpired more than Connie Fortney.

"Tony cares deeply about helping people," she says, "people that have worked hard all of their lives. We say it bold and loud that we help people safeguard their money. It's their money, not ours. Tony is someone they can trust."

Through the years Fortney has been with Tony, one of her responsibilities has been helping to coordinate their annual "Client Appreciation Events." It's at these events that Tony invites his clients to enjoy a meal, entertainment, and prizes. He does it, not because he has to, but because he wants to show his appreciation for their business and their trust.

"He truly enjoys meeting with his clients," continues Fortney. "He does a lot of things he doesn't have to. He was already doing the "Appreciation Events" when I came onboard."

In the beginning, such events were held at Beech Bend Park in Bowling Green. "We took lots of hot dogs and crock pots there," says Tony. "In more recent years, The Belle of Louisville and Churchill Downs in Louisville, three motor coaches with clients from Bowling Green to congregate with clients in Louisville at the Marriott, and Malones Restaurant in Lexington, have been places we've used to show appreciation to our clients."

The hiring of more people coincided with the continuing growth in numbers of clients. It was a simple decision for Tony. The additional employees gave him time to do what he does best, meet a lot of people and sell his services to Savers who are looking to beat their financial worries.

Connie Fortney recalled that a noticeable change began to take place in the business when Tony signed on to be a part of a program called Strategic Coach, in 2002.

For three straight years The Strategic Coach Program required Tony to fly to Chicago once a quarter for the one-day session geared to entrepreneurs meeting with others. Dan Sullivan, a Canadian, and creator of the Coach Program, receives a lot of credit from Tony reshaping his business philosophy.

"Besides the Coach Program, I was in conferences all the time," says Tony. "I studied under Brian Tracy in San Diego, Ed Slott in Atlanta, and my all-time-favorite of coaching were multiple training meetings with the founder of Leap Systems, Bob Castiliogne."

These multiple conferences, along with Tony's willingness to learn new and innovative ways to serve his clients, led to many of the business ideas he has today. "It brought me to a more professional focus. I was getting scattered and as a result I became more focused on the Savers."

All the years spent on the road and in the air, Tony says was time and money well spent.

As someone who doesn't let the grass grow under his feet, it seems that Tony's aim is to cram thirty hours a day into twenty-four. As he likes to say, "It's hard to get a lot done when you're asleep." Besides the many hours spent working on his business and helping his clients, Tony was also busy at his local church, Living Hope Baptist Church in Bowling Green. In addition to serving for three years as a deacon, he also led a men's Bible study for seven years and taught and preached on occasion at Grace Community Church as well.

"I love preaching and teaching. It taught me to keep things simple and try to limit your time while teaching because most people have a very short attention span," Tony laughs. "I try to get the point across in eighteen minutes instead of the usual thirty minutes."

Not far behind Connie Fortney in the office came Heather Hughes. In 2006, she was a stay-at-home mom with two kids, who had moved from St. Louis back to Bowling Green with her husband. With an accounting degree from Western Kentucky University that had enabled her to do some office work for the St. Louis Cardinal baseball team, she knew when coming back home she wanted to re-enter the work force.

"I saw an ad in the paper Tony ran looking for someone with a tax background," Hughes said. "He wanted a person to do research, so that's where I started."

She found herself a few years later, in 2012, of being on the ground floor of developing a software program for Tony Walker Financial.

"It was a game changer as far as what we could give clients," she said about the new program. "I picked up quickly the whole process of retirement."

In 2018, Hughes approached Tony about becoming a fiduciary. With the company's growth and Tony being stretched in all directions, he was receptive to adding another high caliber advisor to his staff.

"When I came to work here, I didn't know what a fiduciary was, but I had listened to Tony for years talk to clients," she added. "I had heard all of the questions to ask and the answers to give."

Tony still takes all of the initial phone calls in his office dealing with retirement. That's how he has built his business and what he does best.

"I do many of the follow-up calls, making sure the client's questions are answered and to see if they are ready to move forward," Hughes says.

With Tony Walker Financial trending upward in Bowling Green, Louisville, and Lexington, and every single applicant originating in the Bowling Green office, Hughes has become the point person.

"I wear lots of hats here," she continues. "Tony is very good at getting the opinions from a very strong staff he has put together. This will become a legacy business, because he has put people in the right place that will make sure Tony Walker Financial is still here years from now."

Chapter Eleven
"IN ORDER TO GROW A BUSINESS, YOU MUST KEEP INVESTING IN YOURSELF AND IN OTHERS AROUND YOU."

Now producing professionally, polished thirty-minute TV and radio shows in Kentucky's three largest cities, Louisville, Lexington, and Bowling Green, Tony had grown his staff to seventeen people.

"We had to hire additional staff just to keep up," he said. "Everything was still being coordinated out of our Bowling Green office, but I was spending at least two days a week or more if needed, in Louisville. And with Lexington now gaining traction I was in that office, too."

That's where Tony's favorite son-in-law, Trey Jurgens and his favorite nephew Wes Walker, Marty's son, have made their presence felt.

Learning the business, with each of them becoming a fiduciary, has done exactly what Tony had hoped for, giving them an opportunity to learn how to do business the right way, and how to help more and more Savers worry less about money.

Now with Heather Hughes, Trey, Wes and Tony as salaried fiduciaries, the business was spreading its base. And unlike other firms who tend to have advisors assigned to various clients, Tony Walker Financial is unique in that they take a team approach. It had become evident months before that Tony couldn't do it alone, and if Tony Walker Financial was to grow it was necessary that he duplicate himself.

Years earlier, Joe Barber, a client of Tony's who had extensive experience in management, wrote a note to Tony encouraging him to bring on more staff in order to grow the business. That advice never fell on deaf ears as Tony recalls, "I had tremendous respect for Joe and so glad I took his advice to learn the art of delegation and finding people who could help with the mission of helping as many Savers as possible."

His move to a larger, easily accessible office on Industrial Drive in Bowling Green, coupled with the statement-making office on Shelbyville Road in Louisville, plus rented space in Lexington, gave Tony Walker Financial the ability to service a large portion of the state.

Continuing to reside at his home in Bowling Green, Tony purchased a second home in Louisville. "I was spending so much time in Louisville that Susan and I bought a home not far from the office," he said. "It doesn't hurt that the new home is conveniently located next door to our grandkids."

With all of the expansions and additions to his business Tony has never forgotten who brought him to the dance in the first place, his clients. "I will always remember that the success of Tony Walker is solely based on the trust and confidence my clients have placed in me and my company. Not only is it an honor to handle their money, but a privilege that I do not take lightly. Lord willing, I don't ever plan on slowing down and making sure there are people in place to continue to serve their needs long after I'm unable to do so."

Tony made sizable investments as well as adding much needed staff, and now he felt was not the time to slow down. Somehow, he would have to find a way to add a couple of extra hours to each day in order to stay ahead with what he had created.

Keeping in mind that man's biggest financial fear is running out of money, which has been the basis of Tony's business plan from the time he was no longer a part of his father-in-law's insurance company years before, he would not venture from his goal.

"I give God all the credit, as He has instilled in me a hope in my future that I declare will not be based on my past," he said. "The unique experiences of my past are past, yet the things in my future are yet to be seen."

It's the fear of the future Tony sets out to talk about with his clients. It's one of the reasons for his recent best-selling book, *Live Well, Die Broke*.

As Tony puts it, "People are sometimes afraid of getting off their wallet and enjoying things they really want to do. My thoughts, don't be afraid to use and enjoy it while you can and for goodness sake, don't rule out getting some of that Mailbox Money® in place so you won't have to worry about running out. While we must certainly plan for tomorrow, we must also learn to live for today."

Over the years Tony has heard at least one good story from his more than 3,000 clients and a few from those who chose to go down another path.

One of those stories puts how people view money in perspective.

"A client of mine owned five cars. He and his wife had totally different views on those cars," said Tony. "As we visited one day, she began talking about how her husband was getting too old to drive and needed to start thinking about selling a few of those cars. Her husband was quick to say he couldn't sell any of the cars as they were worth over $125,000."

"That's the whole point," exclaimed his wife. "You've got over $125,000 sitting out in the barn when we could be using and enjoying some of that money."

"The husband pointed out how much he has invested in the cars and how much he likes to polish and drive them around. I've got my life's work in them," he told Tony.

Moral of the story: money to the client meant little in comparison to his five cars. In his way of thinking, to sell the cars would have been like getting rid of a part of himself. To him, it wasn't about the money.

One of the unique takeaways from Tony is what he has learned in meeting over the years with more than 15,000 Savers: Each client that does business with Tony Walker Financial has to decide how important money is to them. "It's their money," Tony says. "It's up to them to decide how they want to spend it."

Besides focusing only on the Saver personality, Tony also is very focused on the age at which most Savers can take advantage of his services. In fact, the vast majority of Tony's clients are over the age of 60, folks who are already retired or thinking of retiring in the very near future.

All of this plays into the narrative Tony has been saying throughout his career.

"There are a lot of people I meet in this age range of retirement who are under the impression that you have to have millions of dollars in order to retire," he says. "The problem is that they have bought into the narrative controlled by Wall Street that most people do not have enough money to retire, so therefore, you need to keep saving and stockpiling your money with them." Tony goes on to remind the Saver of this truism: "Remember, if you take your money away from Wall Street that means more for you and less for them. No wonder they don't want you to spend and enjoy your money."

But here's the part Tony wants to get across to clients and potential clients.

"Most people I meet do have enough money to retire," he says. "Or at least they can slow down. It might look a little different from what they envisioned, but they can make it with a little help, planning, and guidance from someone who understands money."

This further points out that it is the Savers and not the mega Investors Tony is trying to attract. While more and more financial advisors are now talking about annuities today, it wasn't always like that.

"Years ago, I was raked over the coals by many in the financial world who knew I was a big proponent of annuities. Today it seems like every advisor is talking about them," says Tony. "And it has increased competition for sales. Several years ago, when I was doing annuity seminars, fifty to one hundred people would attend. Then it began to slow down, which is why our main form of marketing our services today is via TV and radio, plus a new presence on social media. We don't do seminars anymore."

Tony, still trying to keep his edge, decided one way he could would be through high level service to his clients. He knew that if he could accomplish this it wouldn't take long for his clients to generate more referrals. He knew to keep the energy up, not just his, he had to have a staff that was just as eager as he was. In order to do that, in 2004 he went to a four-day workweek.

"I want them to be fresh, alert, and ready to provide a service no one else can match," Tony said.

Friday is the day Tony Walker Financial begins each weekend.

"I owe it to my staff to give them a good work environment and pay them well, so when they come to work on Monday morning they are ready to go."

Tony's dad (in sunglasses) as a social worker at Kentucky Village in the late 1950s.

Tony's dad played with the University of Kentucky marching band. He always said he "played for" Coach Bear Bryant in two bowl games, lol.

Tony's mom and dad (pictured in back) were in a popular dance band in the early 1960s. His dad played the saxophone and his mother was an accomplished piano player.

Tony's dad getting his first "big job" heading up the local Children's Bureau in Lexington.

Due to health issues, Tony's dad was forced into early retirement, something that allowed Tony to see at a young age how quickly things can change.

Paycheck stub of Tony's grandfather in 1965. It didn't take much to live on back then.

Tony, or Tony Balony as his friends call him, as a kid in 1965.

Tony and his brother, Marty, with their dog, Cookie, 1964. Tony would later write and publish a children's book called, "The Adventures of Tony Balony and Cookie".

Tony at age nine and his older brother, Marty, getting ready for the big game. Marty was the catcher while Tony pitched.

Southern LL Features Balance

The Lexington Leader, Lexington, Ky., Friday, June 20, 1969

By DICK MILES
Leader Sports Writer

Kiwanis Field in Southland has long been the site of exciting Little League games, tight pennant races, and powerful all-star teams. This year proves to be no exception.

The season thus far has produced some thrilling encounters, the games often going down to the last inning before the outcome is decided. Upsets have been frequent.

The Cubs are presently leading the league in the standings, but they have been defeated twice by the fourth-placed White Sox.

Four teams have a clear shot at the league title, all being within two games of each other. The next two weeks should decide the winner, with the Cubs and Rebels given the edge at this time.

The main reason for the closeness of the race has been the overall balance of the league. No one team dominates play, and with the exception of the weak-hitting Cardinals, each team is capable of defeating any other.

Cubs On Top

The Cubs, atop the league standings with an 8-3 record, are a ballclub characterized by team play. "We have no one player who we rely on," said Cub coach, the Rev. Don Herren, "Every player contributes to our victories."

Pitching and defense have appeared to be the strong points of the Cubs. In Darrell Hoskins, the Cubs have one of the League's top pitchers, while Mark Herren, along with Hoskins, gives the team power at the plate.

Coach Herran is high on his nine-year-old pitcher Tony Walker, whom he thinks will become one of the league's best in the next three years.

"He came during the fourth inning Tuesday against the White Sox and gave up just one unearned run the rest of the game," Herren said. "I'd call him the next Rick Derrickson." Derrickson, who recently signed with the Cleveland Indians, was a Southern Little League star around 1962.

The Cubs major threat to the league title will probably come from the second-place Rebels, who are one-half game behind them at 8-4, as of Tuesday. The Rebels have the fastest pitcher in the league in Steve Bowers. Their strong hitting is headed by Bowers and Billy Knight, both in the league's top ten.

Tony, at age nine, was featured in the local Lexington Leader newspaper about his pitching prowess.

Title A Tossup For Two Southern League Teams

The Lexington Leader, Lexington, Ky., Thursday, June 18, 1970

By DICK MILES
Leader Sports Writer

Anyone who thinks that experience is the only key to success in the Little Leagues should talk to coach Russ Hiten of the Southern Little League Cubs.

Hiten took a team with only two returning regulars this year, a club picked to finish last by many Southern League followers, and guided them to a 8-4 record and a tie for the top spot.

River Raises Purses

CINCINNATI — Purses at River Downs have been raised to a minimum of $1,500 after horsemen refused to enter their horses unless their request for an increase was granted.

Following the announcement of the raise by Director of Racing Kenneth C. Plattner, the entries were quickly filled.

Last Friday track officials and the local committee of the Ohio Division, Horsemen's Benevolent and Protective Association, had agreed to a compromise under which the minimum purses for races at a mile or more would be increased to $1,500, while purses or races at shorter distances would remain to a $1,400 minimum.

The rank - and - file horsemen, though, rejected their committee's recommendation and instituted the entry boycott.

Even before the dispute, purses had been raised from the $1,300 minimum with which the meeting started on May 14.

It is estimated that the increase will mean a jump in purses of about $64,000 over the remainder of the 100-day session, which will close on Labor Day.

Pitching is the strong point for the Cubs, and their duo of Jeff Jervis and ten-year-old Tony Walker ranks among the top in the league. Mark Offutt also handles some of the mound duties.

The last two or three games, however, Cub hitting has picked up, making them a more balanced ball club. "We've been working on our hitting to get it to what I think it should be and it's really coming around," Hiten commented.

Leading the Cubs at the plate has been Jervis, who sports the loop's top average at .484. He has received solid backing from catcher Steve Patterson, while the Mattingly brothers, Mike and Tom, have also been tough.

Tied with the Cubs for top honors are the Yankees, a team which is far different from their first place cohorts.

The Yankees are a defensive ball club which relied on its fielding in the early going. Lately the hitting has picked up, making them a more balanced team.

Coached by Ed McKinney who is in his ninth year with the league, the Yankees are a very experienced team, starting seven 12-year-olds and having to pick up only three players in tryouts. They have been led by Mike Blair, a hard hitting catcher with a .321 average.

Giving the Yankees added batting strength have been shortstop Mark Clifford and first baseman Jimmy Spivey along with John Thomas and Bob Eason.

Pitching for the Yankees has been good throughout the year, especially the efforts of their top hurler, Clifford, Spivey and Hubert Fugate have also thrown well.

In second place, and only one game behind the leaders, are the Rebels. A perennial Southern League powerhouse, the Rebels are coached by Don Ecton.

Strong Hitting

The Rebels are a well balanced team, with one of the strongest hitting attacks in the league. Their lineup features shortstop Billy Knight, the league's second best batter with a .406 mark and second baseman Bobby Silvanik who is close behind with a .405 average. Bobby Mitchell, who owns a .364 average, gives the Rebels another powerful bat.

The Rebels are a young team which had to pick up eight players in tryouts. This fact has failed to dampen the hopes of coach Ecton, who flatly states that "there is no doubt in my mind that we're going to win the title".

In third place are the White Sox and the Braves, both of whom have 5-7 records.

The White Sox have one of the league's better hitters in first baseman Reg Underwool, who has a .351 average. Robby Jones has a .324 mark and handles some of the pitching chores while Allen Bowman is their main moundsman.

The Braves have a strong hitter in Danny Haney, who also doubles as their number one pitcher. Bo Fucci and catcher Mark McCauley have also played well for them.

The Southern League's bottom team, the Cardinals, have a 3-9 record. Led by pitchers David Day and Ricky Arnold, the Cardinals have played well on some occasions and have lost some close ball games.

—F. T. P.

Tony, at age ten, is tapped to be one of the Southern Little League's best pitchers.

Tony, pictured in the middle of the front row, as an 11-year-old on the Little League's All-Star Team. Sadly, they would lose to Gardenside Little League, who went on to the Little League World Series.

Tony as a sophomore at Bowling Green High School, following his baseball team's District crown. They would go to the state tournament that year, losing a heartbreaker to St. Xavier High School, 2-1.

EXPECT THE BEST

Tony's biggest obstacle in 1977 was his team going up against the number one rated team in the country, DeMatha Catholic High School, played in Freedom Hall.

Tony's speed on the basepaths is featured in the local paper.

Tony chilling out as a teenager at his Granddad's place in Troy, Kentucky, 1976.

Susan beside Tony's favorite VW Beetle, given to him by his grandfather, 1976.

Tony and his high school sweetheart, Susan, at their high school prom in 1978. She would go on to be his wife of 40 years and counting.

COLLEGIATE
PAINTING SERVICE

INTERIOR & EXTERIOR

"**5** YEARS" EXPERIENCE

SPECIALIZING IN RESIDENTIAL PAINTING

COLLEGIATE PAINTING SERVICE IS A SUMMER SERVICE COMPANY OPERATED BY TWO UNIVERSITY STUDENTS. OUR GOAL IS TO PROVIDE THE CUSTOMER WITH QUALITY WORK AT A COMPETITIVE PRICE. AFTER SUCCESSFULLY SERVING THE BOWLING GREEN COMMUNITY LAST SUMMER, WE ARE LOOKING FORWARD TO INCREASING OUR SERVICE TO YOU THIS SUMMER.

> WE HOPE WE CAN BE OF SERVICE TO YOU THIS SUMMER.
> IF YOU WOULD LIKE THIS SERVICE OR HAVE ANY QUESTIONS,
> PLEASE CALL ME AFTER 5:00 P.M.
> **TONY WALKER** *843-6773*
> (WKU, BROADCASTING & PSYCHOLOGY MAJOR) **843-6823**

SERVICE INFORMATION:
- REFERENCES UPON REQUEST
- FREE ESTIMATES
- INTERIOR & EXTERIOR
- SATISFACTION GUARANTEED

Thank You for Your Attention!

Flyer (1981) that Tony would stuff into neighborhood mailboxes to spread the word about his painting service.

Tony doing his thing in 1982 at WFKN Radio in Franklin, Kentucky.

```
July 7, 1983

Tony Walker
1310½ Euclid Ave.
Bowling Green, KY  42101

Dear Mr. Walker,

Thank you for responding to our ad!  I have reviewed
the materials you sent and regret to tell you that it
wasn't quite what we were looking for this time out.

All the applicants for this position were very good
and we appreciate you taking the time to let us know
about you.

Good luck in whatever you decide to do.

Best regards,

Gregg Lindahl
Operations Manager

gl/mb
```

Tony "strikes out" trying to find work in the broadcasting field, 1983.

Tony and his wife, Susan, when she worked nights at the local hospital, 1983.

One of many prayer breakfasts orchestrated by Tony. Seated to Tony's right is Joe Foss, a great American who was featured in Tom Brokow's book, "The Greatest Generation".

Tony sitting on the back porch with his late father-in-law, Bill Moore. It was Mr. Moore who gave Tony his start in the financial world.

Tony at the Storer Cable studio, 1998. To his right is cameraman Chris Bratton.

Tony at the Storer Cable Studio in 1996. That's producer Sheryl Morris on the far left.

Tony with the producer of his show, "Your Money Matters," seated behind him is Sheryl Morris, 1996.

Business leaders who spearheaded the First Annual Bowling Green Mayor's Prayer Breakfast. Pictured front row, l-r: Bill Wimberly, Bob Aldridge, B.J. Booth, Adolph Coors IV, Johnny Webb, John Holland, David Garvin, and Bob Fitch. Back row: Barry Bray, Jerry Fondren, Alan Palmer, Steve Cavanaugh, Jimmy Hendrick, and Frank St. Charles.

The first ever Bowling Green Mayor's Prayer Breakfast with over 400 business leaders in attendance.

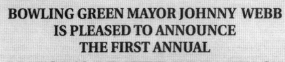

**BOWLING GREEN MAYOR JOHNNY WEBB
IS PLEASED TO ANNOUNCE
THE FIRST ANNUAL**

MAYOR'S PRAYER BREAKFAST

DATE: November 10, 1993
TIME: 7:00 to 8:30 a.m.
PLACE: Greenwood Executive Inn
SPEAKER: Adolph Coors IV

Adolph Coors IV

ABOUT THE SPEAKER: Adolph Coors IV is the great-grandson of Adolph Herman Joseph Coors, who in 1873 founded the world-famous Coors Brewery Company, located in Golden, Colorado. An active member in the family-owned brewery for six years, Mr. Coors left the family business in 1979 to pursue evangelistic ministry. He has served on the Board of Directors of Prison Fellowship, an international prison ministry founded by Chuck Colson. He presently serves on the Advisory Board of the Family Ministry of Campus Crusade For Christ and other Christian based organizations.

Mr. Coors is a frequent speaker and has conducted numerous Prayer Breakfasts, such as the one to be held here in Bowling Green.

He has a fascinating story that challenges every listener to discover the real meaning and purpose of life.

**FOR MORE INFORMATION, CALL:
781-2360, ext. 101**

With no idea who might show up to hear from the great grandson of a beer distributor, Tony proceeded to advertise for the prayer breakfast.

EXPECT THE BEST

Tony was recognized in 2013 as one of the top retirement planners in the country, seen here in the back row (center) of "Senior Market Advisor" magazine.

Tony speaking to a room full of advisors about his work in the field of annuities.

> Dear Tony,
>
> We enjoyed meeting with you last week and we can understand your concern about the securities issue and how it may affect yourself and those in your clan. (Business)
>
> You are a successful person who seems surprised by your success. This is an important part of what and why you come across with trust as well as wisdom.
>
> My advice is move ahead and change what is required. This should not affect the trust that people place in you nor the wisdom you possess.
>
> IF IT WERE ME I would continue to look forward with new ideas and approaches. Reinventing yourself as you go. The issue then becomes how to avoid outpacing your own success.
>
> How to balance what is, with what will be is a problem that faces successful individuals and corporations as well. How do you continue to move ahead without losing touch with the past? How do you continue to support more and more business with the same quality and service you provided to those you served along the path you traveled to success.
>
> I think the key is in the organization you must create to grow. How do you add organization and continue the passion and service of the creator? This eventually becomes the Tipping Point. The link between the past and the future. The point that seperates progress from decline.
>
> I know you are tired at times. I know you want things done quickly and correctly. You can't be everywhere at once no matter how hard you try. The solution is your organization. That is your answer.
>
> Take care Tony. Give us A CALL.
>
> Joe = Brenda Barber

This note of encouragement from Joe Barber, a client with extensive management experience, helped convince Tony that additional team members and learning to delegate would be instrumental in the continued growth and success of Tony Walker Financial.

Tony with his group of fellow Bible Study members, a class that Tony taught for seven years. Tony is pictured second row, second from left.

Pictured l-r: Graphic Artist Deric Hudson, Tony, and the producer of the Worry Free Retirement TV show, Aaron Orrender.

While more of a "ball-golf" guy, Tony's firm sponsors several disc golf courses in the area.

Tony on the set of "WAVE Listens Live" with host, John Ramsey, 2010.

Tony showing off his many industry awards, evidence of his personal annuity production and national recognition. To date, Tony has personally written over 3,000 annuities, totalling nearly $600 million in premium.

As the author of his best-selling book, "Live Well, Die Broke," Tony treats his son-in-law Trey (left), brother Marty (center), and son Anthony (far right) to a round of golf at Pebble Beach.

Tony hosting his radio show on WKCT Radio.

Tony on WKCT Radio talking about one of his books, "Don't Follow the Herd".

Still old-school, Tony writes a personal thank you note to a new client.

An avid reader, Tony proudly displays all of the many books that have helped him shape his unique philosophy on man, money, and God.

Tony's favorite nephew and fellow fudiciary, Wes Walker, checks account balances for a Tony Walker Financial client.

Tony addresses the team during their annual planning retreat.

Tony's media buyer, Gina Tutwiler, discusses the latest TV and radio station commercials with the firm's Chief Compliance Officer, Trey Jurgens.

The original meeting place for Tony and Louisville clients from 2006-2014.

Tony conducting a weekly income planning department meeting in the Bowling Green office.

Tony goes over the actions of an involved planning case with some of his staff. That's Tony's favorite son-in-law, Trey Jurgens to his right.

Connie Fortney discusses with Tony several annuity cases that are pending issue.

Tony discusses the upcoming week with his longest tenured fudiciary, Heather Hughes. A business plan is in place that would allow Heather to take over operations of the firm should something ever happen to Tony.

While Tony no longer conducts educational workshops, he was known to host thirty to forty a year just like this one.

Trey Jurgens presents a long-term planning recommendation to prospective clients while Tony watches on.

"Moving Up!" The Louisville, Ky office at 8303 Shelbyville Road, where Tony can see as many as twenty-five clients and prospects in one day.

Tony hosting one of his many Client Appreciation Events—this one on the Belle of Louisville.

Bowling Green, Ky location which currently houses eleven full-time employees.

Tony reads his latest Children's book, The Adventures of Tony Balony, to his granddaughter Ivy's preschool class.

Tony reads his latest Children's book, The Adventures of Tony Balony, to his granddaughter Scout's preschool class.

Tony enjoying some bacon at his mom's house...the same home where he grew up. As Tony likes to say, "life is too short to eat cheap bacon."

Tony and family at his daughter Lacey's graduation from Murray State University. Pictured l-r: Phillip, his oldest son; wife Susan; Lacey; Tony; and his youngest son, Anthony.

It's on those Fridays and Saturdays Tony can be found on the golf course. With long hours crammed into four days, this is where he finds solace and a place to recharge.

Several years ago, Tony met a well-known Kentucky golfer from Louisville, Buddy Demling. For decades, Demling had been a teaching PGA professional, and was often in demand for trick shot exhibitions around the country.

Upon becoming a client of Tony's, a friendship developed with he and his wife that lasted until Demling's death. Tony and Buddy spent a lot of time together on the golf course, and in typical Tony Walker-style, he parlayed some of the golf advice into financial advice he would pass onto others.

"Buddy told me, 'As you get older, move up in the tee box. He said keep the ball in the fairway, and keep the game simple,'" Tony recalled. "Golf and life are very similar and his three rules in golf can transition to life. In other words, make the game of life easier on yourself by avoiding risks and keeping the plan simple."

"Billy Graham even had his take on golf," Tony noted.

"Being on the golf course is the closest thing to heaven on earth," said Graham.

"After a hard day's work, I look forward to golf, even if it's just getting out and walking nine holes by myself," he says. "While I do keep score, I look at golf as those moments when you have that extraordinary shot, the one that keeps you coming back. Golf and life are so much alike; just keep swinging and sooner or later good things will happen."

Tony Walker Financial and golf run parallel. In comparing the two, Tony would probably have given up after three holes if that was his business. But it wasn't, and it's not.

Tony knows only one way. Stay on the course and keep swinging.

Chapter Twelve
"IF YOU'RE HAVING TROUBLE FINDING THE FAIRWAY, MOVE UP TO THE NEXT TEE."

As golfer Buddy Demling says about golf, "Keep it in the fairway, and keep it simple." And as Tony says about money, "Keep your money safe and keep it simple."

But there's a problem: The financial world hates simple and loves complicated.

"The more complicated they can make the world of money, the more likely you are to rely on them to guide you," cautions Tony.

To simplify money and for those who have some, he breaks individuals into three categories: Savers, Investors, and Speculators. "Most people fall into one of these personalities," says Tony. "The key is finding out how you are wired for money and sticking with investments that fit your financial personality."

How confusing is the avalanche of paperwork sent to customers from insurance companies, Wall Street and even banks. When meeting with prospective clients, Tony hears it all.

"Some tell me all of those multiple-page reports are nothing but meaningless numbers that they can't make heads or tails," he says. "Some say they don't even open them."

It's not just what comes in the mail either. The art of confusion also carries over to what is seen on TV and heard on the radio. It seems that everyone is trying to get your attention in order to sell you something . . . material and books.

"My aim is to convince you that Tony Walker Financial knows what we're talking about," Tony says.

Tony quotes Warren Buffett in an effort to cut through all of the financial world's clutter: "Define what you don't know as well as what you do know and stick to what you know."

Without knowing it, golfer Buddy Demling was right in line with Buffett, one of the richest men in the world, by keeping it simple and sticking with what you know.

"The way an individual is wired financially is the key," says Tony. "It's most important when successfully dealing with savings and investments."

Tony continues:

"As a fiduciary, it's up to me to honestly point out money things a client and potential clients may not be aware of. Me and my staff have the experience in this area that the average consumer may not have or even know exist. Our knowledge can go a long way of keeping them out of trouble with their money."

Tony Walker knows he is in a business where he is selling himself first. It's his personality and charm that often opens the door for him to then present his experience, knowledge, and history of results. His skills at presenting Tony Walker Financial are part God-given talent and decades of falling down and getting back up in the financial world.

Never one to think of himself as a one-man walking encyclopedia, throughout his career he has surrounded himself with people considered the best in America.

One of them is Mark Williams, a thirty-year veteran of the financial services business. As the CEO and President of Brokers International in Des Moines, Iowa, it is the company's objective to assist agencies and financial professionals in growing their business.

Williams' company services some 4,500 financial professionals nationwide with live support as well as digital tools in order to submit both annuity and life insurance applications.

Tony has been a client of Brokers International for several years and the relationship between the two has also given Williams an opportunity to see first hand the efficiency of the Kentucky operation.

"The one thing I continually see with the successful financial professionals that we work with is that they have a repeatable process of doing business and providing service to their customers. Tony Walker is one of those," said Williams.

"I flew my team to Kentucky so we could see his business face-to-face as to how he consistently provides that service. It's a well-oiled machine, a process Tony has created himself."

Williams pointed out that Tony's hiring of more service professionals has given him the ability to see and help more clients.

"He's figured out that in order to service thousands of clients with top notch service, you have to have a process, a way to duplicate what you do day in and day out," Williams added.

Shelby Smith is another financial expert Tony has worked with over the years. Smith, who holds a PhD in economics, is the retired owner of BHC in Houston, Texas. It, too, is a company that offered support services and financial products to some 14,000 agents and advisors throughout the country.

Tony is quick to praise Smith as one of the most knowledgeable people in the country when it comes to annuities.

"I met him in 2004," says Tony. "He noticed I had created my WorryFree Retirement® plan. It was something he had used as well in marketing his company's products at BHC."

"I attended several conferences, the same ones Tony attended," said Smith. "He easily stood out as someone who knew what he was doing. I told him what our company could do for him, and we started doing business together."

Tony arranged to visit Smith at his Houston office and over the years, in addition to their business dealings, they have become good friends.

"He does what is good for his clients, and this is sometimes a rarity," Smith points out about Tony. "He gets his clients to sit down and talk about what they are trying to accomplish. Then he tells them what he can or can't do. He's not looking for the sale on the first visit. He's a down-home guy who is faithful to his customers."

Mike Dressander is also a product and service provider in the financial business. Located in Plainfield, Illinois, just outside of Chicago, Dressander's relationship with Tony goes back several years, and much like other top tier financial advisors, the two met at a conference. From the beginning he was impressed with what Tony was doing with his business back in Kentucky.

"My company looks for people like Tony who are at the top of their game," Dressander said. "He is so consistent, and just as important, very creative in his approach to communicating with clients."

The Illinois based company, was so impressed with Tony and how he gathered his clients that Dressander, on occasion has brought Tony in to speak to his people.

It's for this reason that Tony utilized that ability to train some of Dressander's clients throughout the country in how to better communicate to Savers products and offerings that are available.

"Tony's honesty and integrity is what really stands out. If he tells you something it's going to happen," Dressander continues. "He looks for a specific type of client . . . Savers. There's a saying, 'You catch what you fish for.' Tony catches Savers."

One of those relationships that was a result of Mike Dressander's advisor training program, was Tony getting to know David Lucas.

Lucas had gone through Tony's training program some ten years ago and it changed the way he did things in his Little Rock, Arkansas business.

"I used to complicate things until I met Tony," says Lucas. "He has the ability to take complex issues and make them simple. I've spent time with Tony at his Bowling Green office and saw how he does things. I've listened to his presentations and came away with the simplistic way he operates. We've even developed our own software based on what I've learned from Tony."

Another product of the Dressander program is Scott Braddock, from Raleigh, North Carolina. He's known Tony for more than ten years.

"Until I met Tony, I was flying by the seat of my pants," Braddock says. "He is so grounded and down to earth."

Braddock has been in the financial business for some twenty years, and through his association with Tony has taken his business to another level.

"My business has grown due to what I have implemented because of Tony Walker. "He is so realistic in sharing the process he uses with clients," Braddock says. "He has been ahead of the curve, and what makes him really standout is his ethics. Everyone in our business says they are, but Tony really is.

Braddock, who has traveled to Bowling Green several times to meet with Tony, says he has put several ideas in place he's learned along the way, but one of the most basic in working with a client is to take his time.

"Have some patience, get to know what my clients' needs and wants are," offers Braddock. "I don't have to close on the first meeting, not even the second. It may take a third or even a fourth meeting."

Jeff Goodman lives outside of Chicago and has been in the financial business since 2009. But it wasn't until he met Tony in 2013, that things for him began to accelerate.

"I always take lots of notes when I'm around Tony," volunteered Goodman. "He always has a vision and never loses sight of who he serves . . . his clients, who are Savers."

Goodman points to the reputation Tony has among others in the business and that is why he is always open to learning from the best.

"He's a mega producer," continues Goodman. "As a master communicator he can make his presentation in such a simple, concise manner. He also asks very good questions of his clients so that he knows how to provide a solution. With Tony it goes beyond the money. It's also about the clients' needs and goals.

"We deal with clients who are Savers, and Savers don't want to lose money. He is driven to do it the right way. He's built a business that others in the business respect and want to follow the process he has developed. This is so important."

Goodman acknowledges that Tony has a way of implementing two styles of doing business that seem to work well with his clients.

"He's very old school, yet he's also very innovative, someone not afraid to go outside the norm," Goodman says. "He has a gift with the process he has developed that allows him to continue to grow and learn."

Goodman also applauded the four-day workweek established at Tony Walker Financial.

"The clients seem to like it," he says. "And if someone really needs to get ahold of Tony for any reason, they can. I use a lot of what I've learned from him in my presentation."

Chapter Thirteen
"SOMETIMES THE BEST EMPLOYEES ARE RIGHT UNDER YOUR NOSE."

Dick Walker was spot-on advising his two sons, Marty and Tony, years ago, "Nothing stays the same." And by 2023, Tony's business had grown to 3,000 clients and his staff had increased to a level not imagined back in 1991, to seventeen.

In 2018, Tony made another important decision when he convinced a new family member to become a part of Tony Walker Financial.

Trey Jurgens had married Lacey Walker, Tony and Susan's daughter. He had seen up close how Tony was operating his financial business. His exposure to his father-in-law was enough for him to see that he might like to give it a try. He had been around Tony quite a bit while dating Lacey, and it didn't take long to realize when he was anywhere with Tony, that Tony was like a bright light bulb in the room.

Trey had been good enough at playing football at Fort Thomas Highlands in northern Kentucky that Murray State University, at the far western end of the state, awarded him a scholarship.

That's where he met Lacey Walker. Soon after, he left Murray football and joined the student population, concentrating on his studies that included an emphasis in sports marketing to go along with the courtship of Lacey.

Anything to do with sports he was all in. Along the way he built a solid resume: the baseball museum in Cincinnati, interning with the major league Cincinnati Reds, a sports medicine outreach program, and in a regional capacity for Dick's Sporting Goods.

When Wes Walker, Marty's son, graduated from high school in Lexington, the furthest thing from his mind was becoming a financial advisor. It was 2014, and he had plans to play college baseball and, who knows, perhaps reach the big leagues someday.

For two years Walker did in fact play college ball, at the NAIA level in Indiana. Seeing his baseball future would be limited, by the time his junior year rolled around he had become a student at the University of Kentucky majoring in business.

Away from the classroom, Walker dabbled in weightlifting, even becoming a personal trainer. It was assumed that he would lean toward becoming involved in something to do with music. After all, his dad, Marty, was well known throughout Lexington as a drummer with several high-profile bands. And it was his grandparents, Dick and Jo Walker, who had established themselves with music among the country club circuit in Lexington.

"The closest I got was first chair alto sax in middle school," laughed Wes Walker.

Following graduation from UK in 2018, he took an outside sales position with a digital media company. A couple of years later his professional life was about to head in a direction he would have never predicted.

"Tony called me and asked about me coming into the business," Walker says. "Tony being my uncle, of course, I knew how hard he had worked to make the business what it had grown into. I was living in Lexington, and he just opened up an office there."

It was all new to Wes, but he was willing and able. Soon he was familiarizing himself with life insurance laws, securities, licensing, certifications, annuities, and even becoming a certified fiduciary.

"Tony has given me an opportunity to become a part of something big and with his leadership I've had a chance to get into the investment side of the business," Walker adds. "The business is set up with a great system that is geared to really help our clients."

Wes Walker spends time traveling between Lexington, Louisville, and Bowling Green, doing whatever is required to help steer Tony Walker Financial. Knowing that Tony's television show, along with referrals, is the largest driver of business, he stays prepared to handle any inquiries on Monday's, the day after Tony's television show airs on Sunday.

Chapter Fourteen
"THE MOST PRECIOUS AND DIFFICULT-TO-FIND COMMODITY IN BUSINESS? HONESTY."

Tony, by now, had had a bite of the apple of success and he wanted another bite. That's the way the good Lord had made him. Whatever he did he was driven to succeed. He had known what it was like to go to the depths of the business world as he experienced in the early '90s. Perhaps someone else would have folded and moved on in life. But not Tony Walker.

Tony was at the top of his game. While some encouraged him to slow down, he had become more committed than ever to continue what he had started. A new office in Bowling Green, satellites in Louisville and Lexington, radio and television shows across the state peppered his business with new clients on a weekly basis.

With the growth came the need for additional staff to service the new business. But it wasn't just the new business Tony Walker Financial concentrated on. So are those existing clients. Tony is a stickler about abiding by service-after-the-sale. This is a big reason for his success.

"We get lots of referrals from clients that have been doing financial business for years with us," says Tony. "They know we are there for them and that's why they tell friends and family about how we do business."

"Honesty is hard to find in this business," says Mark Grote. "They (Tony Walker Financial) have proven to me they are trustworthy, not greedy."

Joe Musick says, "I would recommend them. I have had positive experience with Mr. Walker. They offer many services and are prepared to answer any questions and address any concerns you present to them."

"Tony and his staff were excellent. They were great helping me rollover my 401(k)," said Ernie Scott.

"Mr. Walker and everyone on his staff that I have dealt with are consistently knowledgeable, courteous, very professional, empathetic, and kind," Linda Johnson pointed out. "I highly recommend this firm."

Of course, servicing existing business requires staff to handle it, and Tony has spent a lifetime building something worth hanging onto. He aims to do it even if he has to cram thirty hours into twenty-four.

Departmentalizing his office staff has permitted better oversight on new and current clients.

Now with four full-time salaried fiduciaries in house, not working on fees and commissions, along with twelve full-time staff to service their clients, Tony Walker Financial has established five departments to make sure nothing slips through the cracks. Those departments include: Annuities, Charles Schwab accounts, Insurance Service Department, The Income Planning Department, Account Services, and Tax Planning.

Some things bear repeating, and in order to drive certain points home with those watching his TV show or listening on radio, Tony does it a lot.

"Not everyone sees or hears every show," he says. I want them to know the importance I put on helping them save their hard-earned money."

That's why he hammers home how valuable annuities are to him in helping Savers come up with a plan where they can't outlive their money. He speaks a lot about his granddad, and his mailbox money, and being worry free when it comes to retirement.

Tony's several books he has on the market cover an assortment of topics in the financial world, but ultimately come back to what's best for his clients who are made up of those looking to save their money, not invest it. His most recent book on money, *Live Well, Die Broke* reminds Savers that you can't take it with you and it is best to have in place a written game plan that allows you to spend and enjoy this money before it's too late.

In dealing with clients, he and his staff recognize the importance Social Security plays in any retirement plan. He wants those doing business with his company to understand the purpose of Social Security and how it originated.

With many company pensions diverted to 401(k)'s, the closest thing to the mailbox money Tony's granddad received was Social Security. Perhaps the most talked about and least understood source of income in retirement, Social Security is not a bottomless money pit.

Even though most retirees have come to expect it, a few don't solely depend on it to meet their financial needs. That's probably a good thing.

In 1935, the Social Security Act was implemented, and when a person reached age 65, he or she could walk to their mailbox and pick up a check they had earned, but more importantly would receive the rest of their lives.

The truth of the matter was the U.S. Government didn't expect most of the population to live long enough to cash those checks. No serious thought was given to a person reaching sixty-five years of age when the program began.

In 1935, the life expectancy in the United States was 61.7 years, averaging men and women. For men it was 59.9, women 63.9. Who knew back then that by 2023, people would still be living at seventy-eight years average. Who would have known about the advancements in medicine and improvements in quality of lifestyle? The federal government sure didn't.

According to Tony, that's why the Social Security System is in trouble.

"Today's worker is contributing to a system that immediately pays his or her contribution out to current retirees," says Tony. "With all the new money simply going to pay the benefits of today's retirees, there is no real savings within the system."

The new system seemed to work well for a few decades, and in spite of some Americans thinking it was a form of socialism, in that the government takes from one and gives to another. However, it wasn't long before a general population just digging out from the Depression, had been sold on the idea that now the government was, indeed, here to help. A security blanket for widows, orphans and retirees had been rolled out.

In the 1930s, desperate times were a plenty. Jobs were few and with little hope for anything that looked like a future, it wasn't a hard sell for the government to convince this same public that their lives would improve. Keep in mind there was a government mind set very few would live long enough to collect their mailbox money. The general public had not figured it out yet.

The basic needs of food on the table, clothes on your back and a roof over your head were the staple of necessity. That never changes. But a job was required in order to meet those basic needs.

"The math never works," Tony says in talking about Social Security. "As more and more people retire, there are going to be less and less people to support the system. In order for it to remain solvent, taxes must be increased or benefits must be reduced. Americans do not seem to want either."

This is where Tony Walker Financial becomes a part of a plan.

Tony encourages any future clients and existing clients to have a vision of what they expect in retirement. He believes those planning retirement should be armed with a clear vision of what they want in life. He thinks staying focused on such a plan will allow retirees to control their money while worrying less about it.

Chapter Fifteen
"THERE'S NO SUCH THING AS A FREE LUNCH."

Is there anyone who has not received an invitation to a dinner seminar to explain and entice future retirees about investing their money?

"It's all a numbers game," says Tony. "How can an advisor afford to buy a complete stranger a $50 dinner?"

Here's how the financial world can afford to host these expensive steak dinners:

- First, mail out five to ten thousand invitations to people who live nearby and fall into the age range of 55-65.
- If only one percent of those receiving mailers responds to the invitation and attends, that means 50-100 prospects to sell to.
- Cost to advisor thus far? Around $5,000 - $7,500.
- Add in the cost of a nice meal for that many people, $2,500 and now you're up to almost ten grand!
- Goal: Convert at least five "buying units" to clients by placing their money in advisor's investments, usually annuities.
- Average sale per buying unit = $200,000 investment.
- Average commission on the sale of an annuity = 8%
- That's 8% of $1,000,000 in sales or $80,000 in commission to the agent selling the annuities... not a bad night's work.
- Taking it a step further, if the advisor is selling assets under management (investments for a fee), gather $1,000,000 of assets at 1.5% per year fees charged = $15,000 a year to advisor, each and every year. Again, not a bad night's work.
- It really does bear repeating that we in the financial world do better when you do better, and still do better even when you do not.

"Don't get me wrong, in theory there is nothing wrong with dinner seminars. Years ago I did the dinners, and they work," Tony says. "But to me the idea of having to coax a prospect to hear about my services with a free steak is a little goofy, when you think about how long and how hard those Savers worked to save their money, and only for a free steak dinner they are going to hand their money over to the first stranger they meet. Doesn't sound like a good idea to me."

For most of Tony's career he has earned a reputation as an expert on annuities. And for good reason. He believes in them. As a fiduciary he feels a deep obligation to protect as much of his client's money as possible, and it's through annuities he knows this can be accomplished.

Financial experts nationwide were jumping on board with annuities as a way to secure enough money for a worry free retirement. Tony was like Secretariat, turning the corner for home in the Kentucky Derby and way out in front. He was ahead of the field.

A financial article in *USA Today* advised readers to consider taxes, and what types and mix of investments will maximize their returns, and social security, if eligible. Make sure, too, it continued, to check advisory fees and compensation.

The article concluded by telling readers if they decide to seek professional help, use a fiduciary who's legally bound to work in their best interest.

Tony Walker Financial deals with the future and the client's money. The company pays little attention to yesterday and where financially the client had been.

"We know that when it comes to annuities one size doesn't fit all," reminds Tony. "That's why we use as many as eight insurance companies in order to put together a WorryFree Retirement®, plus use the many products offered by Charles Schwab for our investments." As Tony is reminded by his late-great father-in-law, Bill Moore, always remain independent and remember that your client is your employer, not the company you choose to put their money with.

Tony has been astute enough to know that when it comes to marketing, in order to make money he had to spend money. Early in his career he put to good use his deep seeded marketing ability.

"I've always believed in marketing," he says. "But, marketing comes in many forms. If it is not done without a well thought out plan and a good message all you do is waste money."

This is where Tony, digging into his natural abilities, ones you can't learn in a classroom, or from making cold calls, made some decision that would forever accelerate Tony Walker Financial to another level of financial advisors in Kentucky and the Southeast.

Implementing a strategy of keeping it simple and using his granddad's lifestyle as an example, propelled a happenchance cable TV interview into a "throughout Kentucky" TV show.

Always keeping his WorryFree Retirement® at the forefront, he launched productions into hundreds of thousands of homes throughout Kentucky. And it wasn't just television either.

Tony backed up the TV productions with a wide range of thirty-minute radio shows as well as newspaper display advertisements promoting the other media outlets he appeared in.

He knows his shows have a loyal following, even with those not doing business with him . . . yet. He is also aware that not everyone's schedule permits them to see every show. However, through the technology of YouTube, full episodes of his shows can be seen at youtube.com/tonywalkerfinancial.

Currently listed below are the television and radio markets that Tony's show, The WorryFree Retirement® are scheduled.

Louisville television:
WLKY, Saturday 4:30 a.m.; WAVE, Sunday 5 a.m.; WHAS 840 AM, Sunday 10 a.m.; WDRB, Sunday 10 a.m. and 11 p.m.

Lexington television:
LEX18, Saturday 5:30 a.m.

Bowling Green television:
WNKY40, Saturday 6:30 a.m.; WBKO13, Sunday 6:30 and 9:30 a.m.

Louisville radio:
The Answer 970 AM, Saturday 11 a.m. WHAS 840 AM, Saturday's, 12 noon.

Lexington radio:
   WLAP 630AM, Sunday 8 a.m.

Bowling Green radio:
   WKCT 104.1FM and 930AM, Thursday 8:30 a.m.

Elizabethtown radio:
   WAKY 100.1FM/103.5FM/105.5FM/106.3FM/620AM, Sunday 7:00 a.m.

Bardstown radio:
   WBRT 97.1FM, Thursday 9:30 a.m.

As thorough as Tony has been in developing and fine-tuning Tony Walker Financial, he knows he will not be around forever. That's why he has put in place a life insurance policy that will more than cover the funding to ensure the continuation of his business. Currently, the business has no debt and keeps plenty of money on hand to meet emergencies. "One thing Mr. Moore taught me is to always have some cash on hand because you never know what might happen in the future," says Tony.

"My plan is to be sure Tony Walker Financial will continue on, long after I'm dead and gone. I owe that to my clients who depend on us to be there not just when they retire, but all the way through retirement." Tony assures his clients, "Our staff and I have worked to assemble a process that has proven to work. You can depend on that."

Chapter Sixteen

"THERE'S NO POINT IN SAVING MONEY FOR THE FUTURE IF YOU DON'T HAVE A PLAN IN PLACE TO SPEND IT."

A central theme in Tony's life has been, "How does he find time to do everything he does?" Even in his college days, while carrying a full load of classes, he spent weekends working at a radio station in a nearby town. Then the summer job of painting houses turned into much more than 9 until 5. It left very little spare time.

Tony, it seemed, had a knack for keeping several balls in the air. Occasionally one might hit the ground, but he was very good at disguising any disappointments or setbacks that popped up in his young life.

Always with a confident gait, his head held high, and a smile on his face, he kept the pedal to the metal, rarely pumping the brakes, all the while ascending the ladder of success in the financial world.

For Tony, each day comes with a promise. His attitude easily transitions to those around him, leaving his staff at Tony Walker Financial with a professional confidence in their ability to do their job the Tony Walker way.

Tony's way, of course, has always been about his clients. Keeping their money safe, their minds worry free, and money delivered to their mailboxes on a regular basis, has served both Tony and his more than 3,000 clients well.

After his failed attempt at becoming a broadcast journalist, Tony had little hope learning anything about money, especially about how to professionally manage it.

"Life is not about how much money you accumulate over your lifetime, but rather how much you are able to spend and enjoy of what you have accumulated during your lifetime," said Tony. "It makes no sense to stockpile money for the future if you don't have a written game plan in place on when you can safely spend it without running out of it."

He can recall defining moments throughout his decades in the business. One of those slammed him in the face like it did the rest of the world on September 11, 2001.

"It was a turning point in my financial practice," he says. "The day the Twin Towers came crashing down, so, too, did millions of my clients' money. It suddenly dawned on me that the money they had entrusted to me was not protected. They lost money, while I was legally still making money due to the fees I was allowed to charge for managing their money.

"Something didn't seem quite right," Tony continued. "I was still making money on my clients' money, while they were losing it. Money managers like to remind clients, 'When we do better you do better.' But what they fail to say is, 'When you do worse, we still do better.'"

To reach this point, Tony had to finally realize professionally that the stock market really does go up and down. He had known that for most of his life, but it was then, and still is, anyone's guess when it will happen. It's frustrating, especially for someone in the business.

"I decided to investigate a new financial product that had been introduced in the late 1990s," he recalled.

That new product was one that had been around for more than a hundred years, the same concept that employers used to guarantee those pensions like granddad once enjoyed, that's right, annuities. Forever after, the proper use of how to help Savers use annuities to guarantee a return on their money changed the life of Tony Walker, but more importantly, his clients.

"With annuities, my clients sleep better at night and don't worry about what the stock market might do the next day," he said. "I call this *Sleep Insurance®*."

Tony actually sold his first annuity in 1986, and by his own admission had very little knowledge of the risk and fees associated with the product.

Today, Tony Walker is one of the leading individual producers of annuities in America with over $500 million in premiums. Considered by his peers as an expert when it comes to annuities and, in particular, on how to communicate them in a way the average person completely understands them.

The only entity that issues an annuity is an insurance company. In simple terms, the client pays the insurance company what is called a premium. In return, the company provides a guaranteed monthly income. This is what Tony has built much of his business on . . . Mailbox Money®. The key is that this money comes to you the rest of your life. In other words, you can't outlive it.

Through science and statistics, insurance companies know by close scrutiny they can guarantee lifetime payments. This is something Wall Street and banks cannot do.

"This is why annuities are unlike any other retirement planning tool," offers Tony. "No matter how many times those on Wall Street tell you to avoid annuities, there's a little fact about annuities that they tend to leave out. Annuities are the only investment that can guarantee you will never run out of money."

Tony points out that most employers no longer offer guaranteed pension plans like the one his granddad enjoyed.

"Their only option for never running out of money in retirement is a private annuity issued by an insurance company," he says.

In 2019, according to the Life Insurance Marketing and Research Association, annuity sales were $241.7 billion, a three percent increase over 2018.

With numbers like that, Tony says Wall Street and banks are starting to pay attention as well.

"What they will lack is the planning that goes into the client's specific situation," he says.

And it's that planning, experience, and recommendation that separates Tony from the others.

Tony admits, although he has always been about simple, annuity structuring can become a bit complicated when dealing with a client's needs.

"It can be," he says. "And this is another reason many advisors shy away from annuities. They are contracts that come in all shapes and sizes. This is why any advisor offering them needs to have a thorough understanding of such."

Tony Walker Financial and the team work with annuities every day. They know and understand them.

"As fiduciaries, it is our obligation to do our best to monitor all of the different annuities out there, and know which ones will work best for our clients, given the circumstances Savers find themselves in."

Annuities are designed for Savers. They are not hard-wired for Investors or Speculators. Annuities primary focus are the protection of a Saver's money. Savers love protection. Most are not willing to risk a lot of their money.

"The only bad annuity is the annuity that's not right for you and your specific situation, and that's what we try to prevent," Tony says.

While most of the negative reviews about annuities don't come from Savers who love the guaranteed money, there are some.

"They come from the investment folks on Wall Street and large banks who, in most cases don't sell them," he adds. "In any industry, competitors are going to be more negative regarding something they don't sell."

Early on, Tony described himself as a Saver. "Let's be honest, if I were an Investor or Speculator, I wouldn't be very excited about annuities either. That's because annuities are not geared toward growing your money, but first protecting it. I guess you could say I'm a lot like Will Rogers who once said, 'I am more concerned about the return of my money than the return on it.'"

Some people, Tony points out, are well suited for investments that he refers to as speculative, such as bitcoin, gold, or silver.

"Most of my Saver clients would never consider such investments," he says. "Or at least if they did, they would put minimal money in them."

It was only natural that Tony explore more ways to reach clients and potential clients with additional information to help them better understand their money, thinking the easiest way might be through publications. His earlier college days of writing courses and actually putting it to use with press releases while working part-time at a small radio station, had given him enough exposure and confidence to have a shot at it.

While personally meeting with anyone interested in his services, as only he could do, he has still found time to write books — several of them.

Make no mistake . . . money is confusing to most people. The only thing for sure is that everyone wants more of it. It's like a merry-go-round at the fair. Perhaps it is the most simplistic ride on the midway with horses spinning in a circle. However, take a closer look and see if it can be figured out which is the first horse. Not easy, is it? Money is the same way. Not easy, is it?

Slice away the veneer of the slick pitch salesman attempting to get their hands on as much money as possible and right there will be an America full of unqualified so-called professionals trying to follow the money. It's a tug-of-war with Wall Street the Banks, and Insurance Companies on one side, and Money Managers on the other.

Engrained in Tony's approach is, "It's your money, so spend it!"

"Saving is good, but so is spending," he says. "Enjoy what you have earned, it is rightfully yours. I want my clients to know this, but more importantly understand it. We are proud of the fact that we send millions of client dollars each year back to the client. Needless to say, they like that."

To further supplement what Tony talks about during his television, radio, and seminars, he has for several years backed them up with easy to understand books.

His first book *The WorryFree Retirement*® in 2005, was a result of the meetings he has had with thousands of people. Their biggest worry is the uncertainty of their future, he wrote. With no clear vision of where many of them were headed in life and a lack of direction to even find a path, he cautions readers to avoid financial shortcuts, get-rich-quick schemes, risky investments, and unrealistic windfalls.

In 2010, *Don't Follow the Herd* was published. It was Tony's way of telling readers and clients his detailed views on seven costly mistakes people make with their money. But, more importantly he writes about how to avoid them. Of course, he deals with the "herd mentality" of doing what everyone else is doing with their money.

"Like clueless cows led to slaughter, we give the financial world our money because that's what everyone else is doing," the book says. "The result: we suddenly wake up to discover that they've made more money than we have."

Three years later, in 2013, Tony published *The 3 Personalities of Money*®. He writes that in the financial world there are some who might consider him a weird bird. "That's because I'm one of the few financial advisors in the country possessing a formal education and experience in both psychology and finance."

"It's not complicated," he writes. "A person's predominant financial personality is either a Saver, Investor, or Speculator. Once a person determines his or her financial personality, the selection of where to invest is really simple. That's it."

"My two majors in college proved invaluable to the creation of the WorryFree Retirement® process," he says. "The broadcasting and then Psychology, which helped me delve into client's financial personality."

Seeing that Savers were investing in things they didn't understand, Tony came up with an ingenious way to help open their eyes to what was going on with their money.

"I went back to Western Kentucky University, my alma mater, and contracted with two psychology professors to develop a five-minute online quiz that people could take in order to better understand their financial personality," said Tony. "It gives clients or potential clients a better picture of what products they could invest in that was more suited to them, instead of the one-size-fits-all, cookie cutter investments that the financial world is pushing."

Tony continues to explain.

"The three personalities of money boils down this way: All of us are wired for handling money and thinking about money in certain ways. Some are fine in taking risk, others are not. Some love annuities, some do not. Some people are big into real estate, some people are not. It's just the way it is."

(To determine your financial personality log into the free quiz at https://3Personalities.com.) The test is free and only takes about five minutes to complete.

Tony, in 2020, wrote an attention-grabbing book titled *Live Well, Die Broke*. He goes so far to dedicate it to Savers. He says these are people who have worked hard, saved hard, and deep down, have one simple goal in mind: to use and enjoy the money they have worked to save. He is quick to say, "Whether you have a little or a lot, you can still enjoy life."

This is a book that is solid in its writing, examples, and solutions. And unlike other financial publications, Tony doesn't hedge his advice by continually looking for off ramps on the money highway.

Along the way Tony has found the time to write a series of "grab-and-go books," dealing with subjects everybody has heard about, but really know very little.

The six soft-back books fall under what Tony is all about . . . "Made Easy".

401(k) rollovers Made Easy, Investments Made Easy, Annuities Made Easy, Insurance Made Easy, Retirement Made Easy, and Mailbox Money® Made Easy, are all cut-thru-the-chase publications, informative, and relatively easy to read and comprehend.

Now with ten books, with his name on the cover, Tony Walker has established himself as, not only a prominent national financial advisor, but a prolific financial writer.

But wait there's more!

In a humorous sort of way Tony, reaching back to early childhood, has added another book to his portfolio.

In late 2022, *The Adventures of Tony Balony and Cookie* (his dog as a youngster) hit the bookstores, internet, and gift shops. A children's book, of course, with superb illustrations by Chuck Jones, follows a small Tony going through a stage of life learning valuable lessons that hopefully will follow him into adulthood. And while *The Adventures of Tony Balony and Cookie* has nothing to do with money, it does have a lot to do with having fun with your children and grandchildren.

The book gives Tony a chance to show his humorous side and desire to leave a legacy for kids and grandkids everywhere. For more information about Tony Balony and Cookie, log on to www.TonyBalony.com.

Chapter Seventeen
"AT THE END OF THE DAY, IT'S NOT ABOUT THE MONEY BUT ABOUT THE JOURNEY, SO NEVER GIVE UP."

Lexington born with never a real ambition to leave Kentucky, not even for a job offer when he didn't have one. Tony, with all of the self-confidence in the world, chose not to leave.

The truth is Tony probably undersold himself. Even though he never gave up, others wondered what he would do with all of his charm and a face made for television. As he found out later his presence in front of the camera radiated his personality. Still, there is the Kentucky drawl that can, if need be, blurt out a sophisticated "dang it" or a "gee whiz".

An occasional flashback of those cold call selling days help to keep him grounded as a reminder to how far he and Susan have come.

In the '90s the so-called financial advisors were an unknown commodity, lumped in with stockbrokers, insurance salesmen, and bankers. Calling yourself a financial advisor was an opening for the question, "And what do you do?"

Tony found his way through the jungle of managing money. His fierce public niceness has carried him to some 15,000 face-to-face conversations about money. Any of those, some who chose to do business elsewhere, will say there is nothing synthetic about Tony Walker. While some might have the sales pitch of a snake oil peddler, as much as Tony relies on his faith in his personal life as well as his business, he falls way short of coming across as a Bible thumper.

Make no mistake, Tony is a salesman... as smooth as it gets... one of the most successful retirement planning specialists in the country. It would be a mistake to tie Tony to saying or doing anything for a sale. That's why he uniquely puts his fiduciary status at the top of his qualification list.

The orderly manner in which his company goes about their business sometimes borders on infinite. Through the piety of it all he has the ability to blend it all together to where it makes dollars and cents.

Is too much emphasis put on money? When do people know if they ever have enough? Can you ever have enough?

Questions galore about money strangle the airwaves, especially talk radio, seven days a week. It seems that more and more so-called "money experts" are expounding on what is best for listeners. How do they know what to do? Go here. Go there. Go this way. Go that way.

What is so mysterious about money? Why so complicated? Why do people need someone to tell them how to earn it, save it and spend it?

The movement actually began soon after WWII. It was thought that the public now needed help in meeting their financial needs. The late '60s into the early '70s is the time frame credited with the official financial movement establishing itself as an organization that could give credibility to those becoming a part of it . . . The Institution of Certified Financial Planners. It was more than in name only. It actually offered educational programs with criteria to meet the strict standards established.

There will always be a place for financial advisors to exist in order to add value to people's lives and to offer an alternative other than Social Security.

The pace seems to have accelerated in the past several years. Today, with hundreds of thousands of advisors and insurance agents after your money, not to mention all of the advice one can google on the internet, is it any wonder that Savers are dazed and confused about where to turn with their money and who to trust with it.

Tony, through his education, experience, and proven success, is qualified to enable his clients to now because of the money they are able to keep, feel better about where they are in life as it pertains to their future. He had done it through a deeper connection with his clients that meets their heightened expectations. Ultimately, Tony's mission is to offer his clients financial advice, knowledge, and the resources needed to live the lives they desire.

So why doesn't everyone use a financial advisor?

Some think their perceived cost is more than they can afford. Others feel that they don't have enough money to warrant one. And then many are of mind that their finances are simplistic enough to handle it themselves.

Reaching back to Tony's friendship with golfer Buddy Demling, first as a client and then sharing stories on the golf course, it was all about understanding golf and money, and how to be successful with both.

Knowing how to accumulate money is perhaps the most difficult thing to do for anyone trying to create wealth. But keeping it simple like Buddy Demling says, as you get older move up in the tee box. Don't do something you can't. Saving money might be compared to losing weight, eat less and exercise more . . . spend less than you make.

Identify your assets and income, list your debts, and finally tally up what your expenses are to live a quality life. This is where Tony Walker and his team can come in and, using golf terms, tell you what club to use and if you need to move up in the tee box in planning your retirement.

The challenge is for income to keep up with inflation. Taxes are another issue. Knowing that tax codes can be changed at the whim of the federal government is just one more wrinkle in hanging on to money earned.

Statistics reveal that eighty-to-ninety percent of those who start out as financial advisors fall by the wayside after only three years.

Once Tony decided this was where he wanted to be in life, he took his hopes and dreams and laid out his plan. The good thing to it all is there are no expiration dates on them.

What Tony Walker has done in this business is amazing. It can be overwhelming and stressful to identify clients and close them. His staying power has made him one of the top financial advisors in the nation.

With lots of dead ends it takes on the appearance of an elaborate corn maze.

Money is involved in every facet of life. Its consensus definition calls it an official authorized medium of exchange. It can be spent immediately or saved to use later. The later is where Tony Walker has labored for more than thirty years to fine tune his experiences into a well-oiled team of financial advisors that have accumulated more than 3,000 success stories for Savers who never want to run out of money in their retirement years.

There are lessons to be learned about money, and fortunately for Tony's clients, he has learned them. The majority of his clients have done a good job in earning money. But now they have turned to Tony Walker Financial for advice on how to keep it, all the while never running out of it before they die.

Not a day goes by that someone doesn't open a political mailing attempting to sell something, or asking for a donation. Of course, some are worthy, but many don't even come close. Nevertheless, someone is always asking for your money.

An ages-old problem is lack of knowledge about money. Most baby boomers have had to learn the hard way . . . trial and error. Sometimes it worked, other times it didn't.

The sun is finally beginning to shine on efforts being made to reach, even into middle schools, with financial literacy classes for youths. For years, Junior Achievement and 4-H programs have made attempts. But, in order to reach the masses of young people with more positive results, such programs are now being implemented in high schools, sometime jointly being bolstered by community banks and local businesses.

Perhaps what is being taught in high school and college financially through business curriculums will better prepare youths of America for their future that will ultimately lead to WorryFree Retirement®.

Still, most young people are totally unprepared for money issues they will face in the future. A ready, fire, aim approach won't serve them well in life's business dealings.

There will always be uncertainties about money. And that's where Tony Walker has been successful in putting people's minds at ease.

It is here that Tony Walker Financial prepares for the future. With a staff in place, Tony knows it won't be long before the youth of today will be clients tomorrow.

"It's never as bad as you think it is," he says to clients he meets with. "Many of them in doubt about where they are in life financially."

Tony will never put his reputation on the line by making exaggerated promises with regard to a client's money, like some financial advisors do. Remember, he is all about hanging on to the money you have. He will also make sure his clients never try to be something they are not. In other words, Tony always reminds his saver clients "to know thyself" and stay with investments they understand and do not contain inordinate amounts of risk.

As successful as Tony has been, by no means is he ready to plant his flag at the top of the mountain. His achievements, and there are many, haven't fulfilled his one-step-at-a-time approach he set out on back in 1991, when he was only looking for a hill to climb and not a mountain.

The shutters on the camera lens of Tony's mind have opened wide enough for him to see the vision of his future, and to say that he has become an agent of change in people's lives would not be an understatement.

The confidence Tony Walker had as a nine-year-old, firing fast balls past twelve year-olds in the Lexington Little League has never left him. That confidence, added to knowledge, experience, education and God-given talent, has made Tony Walker Financial what it is today.

I guess one could say that the key to Tony's success and that of his company, Tony Walker Financial, is the old adage, "Live for today, plan for tomorrow."

ABOUT THE AUTHOR

Gary P. West has simple criteria when it comes to writing books.

"I only take on a project that I will enjoy writing about and I only write about something I think people will enjoy reading," he says.

West grew up in Elizabethtown, Kentucky and attended Western Kentucky University before graduating from the University of Kentucky in 1967 with a journalism degree. At U.K. he was a daily sports editor for the *Kentucky Kernel.*

Throughout his extensive career he has served as executive director of the Hilltopper Athletic Foundation at Western Kentucky University, provided color commentary for Wes Strader on the Hilltopper Basketball Network, and served as executive director of the Bowling Green Area Convention and Visitors Bureau. He retired from there in 2006 to devote more time to his writing.

He is a freelance writer for several magazines in addition to writing a syndicated newspaper travel column, *Out & About… Kentucky Style,* for several papers across the state. Gary is in demand as a speaker and for book signings throughout Kentucky. This is his nineteenth book.

Gary and his wife, Deborah, live in Bowling Green, Kentucky.

INDEX

A

Adventures of Tony Balony and Cookie, The 69, 95, 119
Aldridge, Bob 80

B

Barber, Joe 61, 83
Beard, Doug 28
BellSouth 16, 24, 43, 44
Bill Moore Insurance 35, 36, 38
Boggs, Mike 28
Booth, B.J. 80
Braddock, Scott 101
Bratton, Chris 47, 79
Bray, Barry 80
Brokow, Tom 78
Brown, Rayford 27
Bryant, Paul "Bear" 17, 65
Buffett, Warren 98

C

Cash, Johnny 33
Cash, June Carter 33
Castiliogne, Bob 58
Cavanaugh, Steve 80
Children's Bureau 23, 67
Collegiate Painting Service (Services) 31, 75
Combs, Leslie 18
Cook, Helen 48
Coors, Adolph 53
Corothers, Danny 27
Cotton Bowl 17
Currens, Bobby 28

D

Demling, Buddy 97, 98, 122
Derrickson, Rick 28
Don't Follow the Herd 87, 117
Dressander, Mike 100, 101
Dubose, Rick 46

F

Fitch, Bob 80
Fondren, Jerry 80
Ford, President Gerald 23
Fortney, Connie 49, 57, 58, 59, 91
Foss, Joe 78
Fucci, Bo 19
Fucci, Dom 19, 20

G

Garvin, David 80
Gibson, Mel 35
Glass, Charlie 25
Goodman, Jeff 102
Graham, Billy 97
Gray, Howard 40
Greatest Generation, The 78
Grote, Mark 105

H

Hardin, Bill 16, 24, 31, 44, 68
Hardin, Eddie 16
Hardin, Hazel 16, 24, 44
Hendrick, Jimmy 80
Henry, Annette 32
Herren, Don 23, 28
Hilliard, Jeff 35, 36
Hock, Chester 35

Hoggard, Bob 27
Holland, John 80
Holland, Monty 28
Horne, Tuffy 29
Hudson, Deric 10, 12, 84
Hughes, Heather 49, 59, 60, 61, 92

J
Johnson, Linda 106
Jones, Chuck 119
Jurgens, Lacey Walker 38, 96, 103
Jurgens, Trey 12, 61, 86, 89, 91, 93, 103

K
Kentucky Kernel 125
Knight, Billy 19
Knight, Bobby 19
Kuralt, Charles 23

L
LEX18 tv 111
Lexington Herald-Leader 28, 70
Live Well, Die Broke 62, 86, 106, 118
Long, Steve 28, 29
Lucas, David 101

M
Madden, Anita 18
Madden, Preston 18
Madison, Keith 29
Mailbox Money® 24, 42, 43, 63, 115, 119
McNeill, Tammy 48, 49
Moore, Bill 34, 35, 41, 52, 78, 110
Moore, Della 34
Moore, General Hal 35
Moore, Jim 35, 36
Morris, Sheryl 46, 47, 79, 80
Musick, Joe 105

N
Nichols, George 27

O
O'Leary, Kevin 44
O'Neill, Tip 23
Orrender, Aaron 10, 11, 12, 13, 54, 84
Out & About...Kentucky Style 125

P
Palmer, Alan 80
Parker, Jerry 39
Parrot, Jeff 19
Pickens, Jim Jr. 28
Pressley, Mike 53

R
Ramsey, John 85
Ray, Felton 27
Renaud, Eldon 53
Reynolds, Kenny 28
Robbins Agency, The 37
Robbins, Bill 37, 38
Robert, Joe 28
Rogers, Will 40, 116
Rupp, Adolph 17

S
Scott, Ernie 105
Sears, Wilson 27
Security and Exchange Commission 11
Sleep Insurance® 114
Slott, Ed 58
Smith, Shelby 100
Solomon, Art 38, 39
South Central Bell 16
Stahl, Mark 28
St. Charles, Frank 80
Stone, Henry 32, 33
Strader, Wes 125
Strategic Coach Program, The 58
Sugar Bowl 17
Sullivan, Cindy 48
Sullivan, Dan 58
Sutherland, Kermit 53

T

The Answer 970 AM radio 111
The 3 Personalities of Money® 117
The Money Missionary® 47
The WorryFree Retirement® 24
The WorryFree Retirement® book 47, 48, 117
"The WorryFree Retirement®" show 48, 111
Thomas, Clarence 28
Thornton, Steve 28
Tony Walker Financial 10, 12, 13, 44, 49, 51, 56, 57, 59, 60, 61, 62, 63, 64, 83, 88, 97, 98, 99, 102, 103, 104, 105, 106, 108, 110, 111, 113, 115, 123, 124
Tracy, Brian 58
Tutwiler, Gina 55, 89

U

USA Today 110

W

WAKY radio 112
Walker, Anita 19
Walker, Anthony 39, 41, 86, 96
Walker Financial 40
Walker Group, The 36, 37
Walker, Harry 15, 19
Walker, Jo Hardin 15, 16, 17, 18, 21, 23, 24, 37, 66, 104
Walker, Marty 15, 17, 18, 19, 21, 22, 23, 26, 30, 32, 52, 61, 69, 86, 103, 104

Walker, Phillip 36, 37, 96
Walker, Richard "Dick" 15, 16, 17, 18, 19, 21, 22, 23, 24, 26, 31, 39, 65, 66, 67, 103, 104
Walker, Susan Moore 14, 29, 31, 32, 34, 36, 37, 38, 39, 40, 41, 45, 51, 52, 56, 57, 62, 73, 74, 77, 96, 103
Walker, Wes 12, 61, 88, 103, 104
"WAVE Listens Live" 48, 51, 85
WAVE tv 10, 48, 49, 111
WBKO tv 111
WBRT radio 112
WDRB tv 111
Webb, Johnny 53, 80
West, Gary P. 7, 125
WFKN radio 32, 76
WHAS radio 111
WHAS tv 111
Whitlow, Brad 27
Whitney, C.V. 18
Williams, Mark 99, 100
Williams, Rick 34
Wimberly, Bill 80
WKCT radio 87, 112
WLAP radio 112
WLKY tv 111
WNKY tv 111
WorryFree Productions 10, 13
WorryFree Retirement® 100, 110, 111, 118, 123

Y

"Your Money Matters" 46, 47, 80